Who's My Daddy?
Exposing the Roots of Family Secrets

A memoir
by
Gina Cameron

Banner Peak Press

Copyright © 2024 Gina Cameron
All rights reserved.
ISBN: 979-8-218-35372-8

For my family and friends who walked this journey
with me every step of the way.

*I am what time, circumstance,
history have made of me, certainly,
but I am, also, much more than that.
So are we all.*
                                    James Baldwin

Preface

The first time my mother compared my skin color to hers, I was thirteen, just home from a Fourth of July beach party in the south Florida sun. It was the early 1960s, long before SPF labels on sunscreen and my skin glistened with baby oil and flecks of beach sand.

"Look how dark you are," my mother said, her tone ominous, as she slid her pale-ivory forearm next to mine. Her voice edged up in alarm. "Much darker than me." My arm was burnished to an olive-hued mahogany.

"I'm getting a tan," I said with defiance as I yanked my arm away. I wasn't sure exactly what I was defying. I only knew I wanted to get away from my mother's scrutiny. And away from a familiar sense of shame, of feeling that somehow there was something not quite right about me.

"Too dark," my mother called to my back as I fled to my bedroom. "You'd better watch out."

In the remaining fifty years of our time together my mother remarked on my skin tone many times. Too many for me to recount. I never sought out the reason behind her preoccupation.

My mother was dead by the time I discovered my father wasn't my biological father.

The fact that she lied to me about my paternity hurt more than the knowledge that I didn't carry my father's DNA. He and I had a contentious relationship and I'd long since put to rest my longing for a close father-daughter bond. Still, I was gripped with a dizzying sense of unreality. The origin of my body was unknown.

I embarked on a search to find the man responsible for my being. I couldn't quite put my finger on why I felt so driven to find him. How would my life change if I knew who he was? I would still be "me", wouldn't I? Yet I desperately wanted to find my biological father.

I wasn't alone in my desire or my quest.

More than twenty-six million people have taken genetic ancestry tests and many have been faced with the facts of a heritage other than they'd expected. The Facebook group DNA NPE Friends (NPE refers to the genealogy term "not parent expected") has several thousand members. Posts are rife with anguished emotions. Genealogy research is now a lucrative business.

What compelled my mother to hide the truth from me for sixty-three years? What compelled thousands of other mothers to lie about their child's paternity?

What drove me and thousands of other NPEs to search for our biological fathers?

My questions took me on an exploration of human evolution, tracing the arch of our history from matriarchy to patriarchy. What I found surprised me and launched me on an unexpected path of healing.

Chapter 1

I was at a family reunion in New York with cousins I hadn't seen in decades. By then we were all in our sixties. My cousin Dan and I were reminiscing about our fathers' shared love of history, how they could discuss, for hours, minute details of the rise of the AFL-CIO or Roosevelt's New Deal.

"Of course, you and your sister have different fathers," Dan said as an aside to the story he was recounting.

"Wait," I said, my body flushed hot. "I've never heard that before. Vicki and I have different fathers? What do you mean?"

"Just that Louie wasn't your dad." Dan shifted in his seat. Clearly, he thought I knew this.

"What else do you know?" I choked out.

"Nothing else." He looked around the room and back to me. "We all always knew. We were told never to tell you, but I thought you knew by now," he said, turning to talk with his son.

We all always knew echoed in my head. My ears thrummed with a deep ocean roar. All around the table, everyone's mouth was moving, but no intelligible words were coming out. I almost stood up to yell "hey, what do you all know about my father?" but caught myself, not wanting to turn the long-awaited gathering towards my own needs.

Instead, I took a deep breath and sat back in my chair. The room was filled with laughter and chatter as barbecue chicken and salads passed hand to hand around the dinner table. The bombshell about my father could wait. I tried to rejoin conversations about children, jobs and travel, but Dan's revelation was all I could think about.

My sister Vicki had planned this reunion of cousins on our father's side in her home when I, visiting from San Diego, could attend. All our aunts, uncles and parents were dead now, and their riffs, estrangements, arguments over money and wills, all that had kept us apart for decades, were irrelevant. I had been excited to reconnect with family I hadn't seen in over thirty years.

Could it be possible this wasn't *my* family reunion?

*

On the ride back to my hotel that night, I remembered overhearing a conversation between my mother and her sister late one night when I was twelve. Refugees from Latvia after WWII, they spoke a mix of their native language and English.

"Louie isn't Genie's father," I heard Aunt Tessie say.

Not my father? I wanted to run out and ask what she meant, but knew I wasn't supposed to be awake, much less listening to the adults.

I clutched that sentence inside myself for days, and finally asked my mother's best friend Winnie if it was true. Why I asked her, and not my mother or aunt, meant I recognized the volatility of what I'd heard. I don't remember Winnie's reaction, only that she must have called my mother as soon as I left and told her what I said.

When I returned home from Winnie's house, my mother stood in the kitchen, a dishtowel wringing in her hands, eyes blazing.

"How dare you?" she said through clenched teeth. "Of course, he is your father. How dare you be so ungrateful? You should be ashamed of yourself."

I was sent to my room, shunned for days by both my mother and father. I buried the possibility that I had heard the truth deep inside and felt guilty for even considering I could have heard correctly, that I could have any doubt about my father. Yet just hours after hearing Dan's news, the memory of that overheard conversation surfaced. I hadn't buried it very deep after all.

My father and I had always had a fractious, distant relationship. I'd spent many years in therapy trying to put to rest my longing for a caring, loving dad. Now here was possible proof that our distance had a far deeper cause than I'd ever imagined.

*

I made plans to meet up with Ellen, my father's niece, a few days after the reunion to take a walk on the High Line in

Manhattan. "Yes, I vaguely remember something about you not being Louie's daughter," she answered my query. "But my sister Karen is seven years older than you or me and she might remember more. I'll call her tomorrow and let you know."

Ellen called me while I was at JFK airport awaiting my flight home. "Karen has a clear memory of a visit to our Grandma Ida, Louie's mother, when she was ten years old," Ellen reported. "Grandma Ida told Karen she had a new cousin. When Karen asked who had had a baby, Ida replied the new cousin wasn't a baby, she was a little girl. You were three years old when Karen met you. Three years old when Louie met your mom."

I felt light headed, leaned against the wall for balance, my voice husky when I repeated "three years old?"

"Karen was very clear about that," said Ellen.

Thoughts crowded my head. Three is such a tender age. The thought of myself as a little girl brought tears to my eyes. I had worked as a pediatric physical therapist in an early intervention program for twenty-five years. I knew the importance of the first few years of a child's life and how perceptive children are by age three.

"Are you still there?" Ellen asked.

"Yes," my voice broke. "Hold on. I need to find a seat."

Three years old? A line from the letter my father sent when he disowned me twenty-four years earlier popped into my head as I found a seat in the terminal. I was forty-two years old when I received his letter.

"You've been a thorn in my side since you were three years old," it said.

Now his letter made sense. I was three when he met my mother. I wasn't his child. He fell in love with a woman and she had an unwanted side-kick – me.

The JFK terminal buzzed with activity and brought me back to the present. Intercom announcements made it hard to hear Ellen, who kept repeating "Gina, are you okay?"

"I keep losing reception," I answered. "I'll call you back when I'm home." Dazed, I felt faint and nauseous. If Louie wasn't my father, who was? And why had my mother never told me?

Chapter 2

I had a window seat on the airplane from New York to San Diego to conceal my tear-streaked face. "You've been a thorn in my side since you were three years old" echoed loud in my head. For decades I'd been mystified and horrified by that sentence. How could a father write that to his daughter? Now I knew. How dare my mother hide the truth from me? Memories of the incidents leading up to the receipt of my father's letter and my subsequent four-year estrangement from my family came flooding back as I traveled the miles home. The scenes rolled by like the clouds outside my oval window.

    I was thirty-six years old and recently graduated from Boston University with a Master of Science in Physical Therapy degree. My husband Walter and I and our two-year-old son, Eli, moved to San Diego. We rented a small two-bedroom house. I got a job as a pediatric physical therapist with a public agency serving children with disabilities. Walter, a licensed plumber, also began work full-time. The best daycare center we could find for Eli was in the opposite direction of my workplace, which required early morning and late afternoon freeway flying. Like most working parents, we were wrung out at the end of the day, but we were satisfied that our small family was thriving.

My parents came to see us several months after we were settled into our new routine. A friend of mine nearby ran a bed and breakfast, which I rented for them for a week. Evenings were spent together at our house, making meals and catching up on our day.

"Do you want to take your bath now or in ten minutes?" I asked Eli, who by then was three years old, with blond curls and bundles of energy. We'd all finished dinner and it was getting late.

"Ten minutes," he called over his shoulder as he ran outside to the yard.

"Since when does a three- year- old get to pick his bath time?" my mother said. "He's three for God's sake. You should be in control."

I took a deep breath, let a few seconds pass. "We like to give him some choices, help him feel he's a part of the decision making," I said, measuring my words. "It's called assertive parenting, not too authoritarian, not too lenient."

"Don't give me any of your psychology mumbo-jumbo." She flashed me a withering look. "You're raising a spoiled brat. I raised you with love and guilt. You should follow my example."

"Guilt?" I asked. "You felt guilty raising me?"

"Of course not," she said. "I raised you so you'd feel guilty."

"Why?"

"I'm your mother. You wouldn't be here without me." She wasn't smiling. Her eyes narrowed behind her glasses. I knew she believed her words held a valuable lesson. I also knew that guilt was the last thing I wanted to burden Eli with.

"What are you and Dad going to do tomorrow?" I asked, changing the subject, pretending not to notice the shift in the emotional atmosphere. I was an ace at sliding out from under confrontation, not swallowing the bait.

Ever since Eli had matured from babyhood to a toddler, developing a will of his own, my mother had grown increasing critical of his behavior. Visits had become predictable. The first day or two were harmonious, my mother bubbly with excitement over her only grandchild. Then Eli would, as kids do, refuse to sit still at the dinner table or demand another cookie or act sullen when asked to clean up his toys. My mother would bristle, and the litany of complaints about his behavior would start.

"You're spoiling him. He has you wrapped around his little finger. You don't see how manipulative he is."

My father was usually a bystander to her outbursts, reading the newspaper. But the looks that passed between them denoted his complicity with her gripes. I was constantly on edge.

I wished I could say I welcomed our visits together as an extended family, that it was important to me that Eli got to know his grandparents. I didn't. It wasn't. I always felt split. Split between wanting a harmonious relationship with my parents, times when we could enjoy each other, and knowing my desire was a pipe dream. I knew my mother and father were individuals, apart from being my parents, who had led interesting lives and who loved to travel. I fantasied that those people would show up at my door, be relaxed, and funny and kind. I hoped that those parents would cherish me and my husband and son, would bestow love and kindness on us, support us in our busy lives, show some understanding. But that wasn't what our times together had been in the past. Criticism and tension were what I could expect. For me, visits were all done out of a sense of duty. Maybe there lived in me still a small glimmer of hope that this time, maybe this visit, we'd connect, really be a family. But the hope was small and each visit proved it futile. I was always on edge, always "performing" for the benefit of my mother especially, and lesser so for my father, because he more and more seemed disinterested in me. He did like Walter, and turned his attention to him. It galled me that my father took their conversations about history and politics seriously, that Walter's opinions mattered, as opposed to mine, which he never sought out and denigrated when I ventured to state them. But I was grateful for the harmony that existed between my parents and my husband. In contrast, the tension between my mother and me was always palpable.

    I had enough insight from my early studies in psychology to surmise my mother's controlling behavior came from her early experiences. It seemed likely that the constant upheaval, adversity and uncertainty she faced as a teenage refugee in Europe during WWII had primed her to try to control her surroundings, especially her family, as a way to feel safe. Being the target of her barbs stung, but I tried to shrug it off. Besides, what was my alternative?

When I was eighteen my mother and I had gone to one family counseling session, at my insistence, a few months after my father kicked me out of the house. My only memories of the session are the sterility of the office, the male counselor, and my copious tears.

"Not my cup of tea," my mother pronounced afterward. "I am who I am. You can't make an old leopard change her spots. Take me or leave me."

I took her, torn between yearning for a close relationship with her and wanting to be as far away from her as possible. But now, her constant picking at my son, which was in effect criticism of my parenting, of me, was chafing me raw.

*

"We're not ready to go home yet," my mother said as we were sitting down to dinner on the last night of their visit. "I called the airline and we can fly back next week instead."

"But your bed and breakfast here isn't available next week," I said, my stomach clenching. "Where are you going to sleep?"

"Here with you," she said, triumphantly.

"Our place is too small for all of us together," I said.

"What do you mean?" Her voice rose an octave. "That's what families do. Stay with each other. Put each other up."

"Someone would have to sleep in the living room," I said. "Mornings are already hectic. We're rushing to get out the door on time for work. I'll find another bed and breakfast for you nearby."

"You don't want me here," she said, her face reddening. "You'd rather I'd just go away."

My father pushed his chair back. No one was eating. Eli was wide-eyed in his high-chair, aware of the rising tension.

"Mom, please, can we decide this after dinner?" I felt trapped. She was right. I didn't want her here, in my home, at all hours, not leaving me any breathing room, not giving me a sanctuary to retreat from her expectations. How could I say that to my mother?

"How am I supposed to eat?" she sniffed, tears welling in her eyes. "My own daughter doesn't want me in her home."

"Ludy, that's not true," Walter tried to pacify the situation. "We all love you."

"Do you think I can't see what's going on?" She jerked her head back, swiveled her chin in my direction. "She can't wait to get rid of me, put me in some stranger's house," she said as she stood up, her whole body shaking, grabbing for the edge of the table to steady herself. "Louie, call a taxi," she said to my father. "I want to go to the airport right now. Right now."

My father didn't move.

"Mom, please," I said, my chest heaving, trying not to cry. "It's late. We'll work something out."

Walter got up, walked around the table, knelt down next to my mother, put his hand over hers. A rush of grief rose up in me at the sight of his compassion, a compassion for her I couldn't summon in myself. Unable to control the heat roaring through my body, the onslaught of tears, I fled the table, ran to Eli's bedroom. On hands and knees, I entered his closet, pushing aside his shoes, a stuffed Shamu from Sea

World, boxes of foam building blocks, and closed the door behind me, wedging myself into the corner. I grabbed for his clothing, burying my face to muffle my sobs.

The next day my parents and their suitcases moved into our house. Walter and I slept on a futon on the living room floor, giving them our bedroom. My mother and I sidled past one another, polite, our eyes downcast. I was in the kitchen, my hands sticky with ground turkey, meatballs sauteing in a frying pan, when Walter walked in, leaving my parents to watch Eli splash in a wading pool in the yard. Walter sighed as he sat down heavily.

"Louie just told me you have always been mentally ill," he said, shaking his head slowly back and forth.

"What did you say?" I asked, tears and anger engulfing me. How dare he blame our family problems all on me, I thought.

"I said I disagreed."

"What else did he say?"

"That he just wanted to warn me. I got up and left him sitting there."

The gist of my father's accusation – that there was something wrong with me – felt familiar, a subtle, and sometimes not so subtle, message he'd given me throughout my life. Confusion once again rattled through me. Why me? What does he see in me that raises his ire? What was wrong with me?

*

A few years later, with a $10,000 gift from my parents, Walter and I bought a home in the San Diego suburbs. We hosted a gathering of my family, my sister and her husband

and my parents. In the middle of dinner, everyone seated around the dining room table, Eli, age five, slid off his chair and ran over to nuzzle next to our new Labrador retriever puppy.

"You're not teaching Eli any manners," my mother said. "Too bad we can't just lock him in the closet. That's what we did to you when you were little and you misbehaved." The words slipped from her lips, her face open and vulnerable for a second. Then she inhaled sharply and lowered her gaze.

A few beats passed, no one saying a word, no one questioning her admission, everyone complicit in the family covenant of buttressing her virtuous status. Walter caught my eye, eyebrows raised. I was blown back against my chair, back in my recurring childhood waking nightmare. Heavy material draped over my face and body. The impenetrable darkness. The cloying smell of mothballs. Waves of terror rushing over me. I wasn't making those feelings up. That hadn't been just a disturbing fantasy. I had been locked in a closet as a small child. My mother just admitted it. My lifelong fear of elevators, of any enclosed space where an exit was not immediately available - here was a plausible cause. I remembered retreating to Eli's closet during my mother's outburst of anger a few years before. Had I unconsciously replayed my mother and father's punishment of me as a child? I sat in silence, engulfed in memories, as the table banter resumed around me.

*

Several months later, my small family and I made our annual trek to visit my parents for Christmas. By then my father was seventy-seven years old. He had trouble swallowing and was diagnosed with bulbar palsy, a neurological disease with no cure, causing weakness of the muscles needed for eating, drinking and managing saliva. Eli was six years old, tall for his age, a lean, active and outgoing kid.

I'd prepared myself for the trip by seeing a therapist, learning strategies to maintain my boundaries, practicing to remember that my mother's control issues were just that, her issues, not really about me at all. And especially not about Eli.

Even so, the visit was just as tension-filled and stressful as subsequent ones, culminating with my mother's proclamation, "You mark my words. Eli is going to grow up to be a juvenile delinquent."

*

After that visit, I couldn't take another one anytime soon. Our usual rhythm was my parents would come to San Diego during Easter, so I cooked up an excuse to head that off at the pass.

"We're going camping with friends over spring break," I said when my mother broached the subject of their trip as expected during a phone conversation. "Not a good time for you to come this year." A long silence ensued.

"Well, so much for your parents," she said, her voice huffy.

"Another time," I said without offering a concrete date.

The phone rang the next day.

"I'm in the hospital," my mother, her voice weak, said.

"What happened?"

"My aorta went into spasm and I had a heart attack."

My fault, I thought. My body flushed hot. She must have been enraged I'd nixed her visit. Could anger cause an aortic spasm?

"What does your doctor say?"

"I'm stable. I'll be fine." Her plaintive tone of voice contradicted her words.

"Do you want me to come to see you?"

"You shouldn't," she paused, "bother," she continued, elongating the syllables.

I grabbed on to her words.

"I'll call you tomorrow."

"What a drama queen," I said to my husband after the call, trying to outsmart the queasiness I felt in my stomach, the creeping guilt at having told an unconvincing lie. She'd sussed me out, hurt by my rejection. See how fragile she was? I hated feeling responsible for her feelings. Now she would blame me for ruining her health, too.

*

"Doris's daughter bought a house nearby, near Doris," my mother said. We were talking on the phone a few weeks after she'd returned home from the hospital. "Doris and her daughter are making drapes for the front window together."

I knew my mother would have preferred a daughter who liked to sew. Instead, I was a bookworm, a non-make-up-wearing political activist. I was too serious, not able to keep up with the conversational banter that was her trademark.

"And you? You had to move so far away?" she continued. "What is it you're doing that's so important?" My irritation began to bubble.

She went on. "Children don't love their parents like they did when I was young. I did my mother's bidding, there was never a question of anything else."

"What bidding?" I said. "What bidding should I have done?"

"I had a heart attack," she said.

"And you said I needn't come."

"Well," she harrumphed. "You're my oldest daughter."

"Mom, please stop," I said. I tried to remember my last therapy session, suggestions for how to stand up for myself against the guilt baiting. "You and I both know we have a problem in our relationship. I'd really like us to work on that, try some counseling together."

Silence for a few seconds. It seemed as if all the air across the entire continent had been sucked into the upper atmosphere. She slammed down the phone. I called back. She didn't answer. A few days later, I wrote a letter, said I loved her and dad and I wanted things to get better. I suggested meeting somewhere neutral, or going to a therapist. I called several times. No one picked up. Just silence, for three months.

The silence gnawed at my gut. I'd been shunned for days before, even weeks. Each time we'd resumed our uneasy dance, not having resolved any issues, but at least still in relationship. I expected this time would be the same. I was wrong.

*

I was ready to take my six-year- old son Eli boogey-boarding near Scripps pier on a Saturday morning, a wet suit in the car. I had my swim suit on when I emptied the mailbox, eager to leave.

The envelope was typed, some letters dark, some faint which I recognized from my father's worn-out carbon ribbon, the "e" off-kilter from the bent rod on his manual Corona. I ripped open the envelope and slipped out a one page, onion-skin piece of paper, typed, single spaced, signed "your father" in the familiar scratch of his handwriting.

"You've been a thorn in my side since you were three years old." The words leapt off the page. "You are mentally ill, inventing slights and problems…there's a sickness in your brain…you are selfish…now you've gone too far…I never want to see or hear from you again."

"Proof. Here it is - proof," I yelled as if torched, flinging the incendiary paper onto the dining room table. "Proof, proof, proof," I intoned, pounding the letter over and over with my flat hand.

"Proof?" my husband poked his head through the kitchen door, eyes wide with alarm. "What happened? Proof of what?"

"Proof I haven't been imagining it," I said. "His hatred for me all these years." I paced the floor, my whole body thrumming with a volcano of emotion. "Look, it's right here in black and white," I jabbed at the letter, thrust it towards Walter. My father's face, locked in a sneer of disgust, flashed before me. The cut of his eyes as he ridiculed the size of my nose. The twist of his lips when he kicked me out of the house. Years of hurt and confusion stoked my eruption. "A thorn in his side since I was three," I spit out each word.

"Mommy," Eli called out as he came down the hall from his bedroom. "Can we go now?" He had his wet suit on, yellow florescent stripes down his belly.

"Give me a minute," I told him, attempting to calm my voice. "Go load the towels and drinks in the car."

Eli at three: how I loved his blond curls, his exuberance. He had a temper tantrum when I refused to buy a mutant ninja turtle sword at the store. His whining request "read just one more Berenstein Bear book" at bedtime had wrung me out more than once. But a thorn in my side? Never.

"How could he write those things?" Walter said, his face pale. "And what's with age three? That's crazy."

I grabbed the letter from Walter, reading further down the page. "Your mother, a simple woman, only wanting her daughter's love." The words flashed neon in my mind, taking me to my knees.

Why had I said those things to her? How had I dared? Thorn, sickness, selfish – my father's words echoed again and again in my head. I had hurt my mother, the worst sin, an abomination beyond belief.

"I'm sorry, I'm sorry, I'm sorry," I keened as I climbed into my husband's lap, both of us on the floor, his arms around me, rocking back and forth.

"You don't deserve this," he said tenderly. "Louie is dead wrong."

My fog of emotion began to lift. I noticed the wood grain of the piano, the hummingbirds woven into the Mexican tapestry, the walls still standing around me. "Eli," I remembered. "The beach."

"I'll take him," Walter said. "I'll call Karen and see if she can hang out with you."

My friend arrived, read the letter, both of us in disbelief. She took me to a secluded beach where the roar of the surf drowned out the ebb and flow of my tears.

"Why three?" I kept repeating. "What happened then?"

*

I took the letter to my therapist. What would she tell me? Would she investigate my role in this attack? Perhaps I was bad after all. I teetered between wanting to believe my husband and berating myself for having said anything to my mother so soon after her heart attack, a sour pit of guilt gnawing in my stomach. Did I deserve this rejection?

"It's clear the foundation of your family was built on the myth that you are the bad one," my therapist said. "Often family systems blame one person, project all the problems on him or her. You are that person in your family. And when you refused to play along any longer, when you stood up for yourself, you pulled out a cornerstone of the family foundation and the whole thing came crashing down."

"Yeah, crashing down on me." I wiped my eyes.

"Now we'll rebuild a new foundation for you," she said, meeting my eyes to let me know she saw me. Saw my history and my pain.

*

Three years passed. During that time, I reached out to my mother once, sending her a photo of Eli, me, and our Labrador retriever all piled together on a bed. I didn't hear back. Then one day I came home to a voice message from my sister on the answering machine. Dad was in hospice, dying. He'd refused placement of a gastric feeding tube to prolong his life. I called hospices in Boynton Beach, found out where he was, spent 24 hours debating whether or not to fly home. What if I arrived at my mother's house and she slammed the door in my face? I had no guarantee I was wanted. I decided to take a chance and go. When I called the hospice again, I found out he had already died. Numb and unsure of what to do, I never booked the flight.

*

"Return your seats and tray tables to their upright positions," the flight attendant announced as my flight from New York to San Diego neared its destination. I pulled myself out of the fog of painful memories. Now a whole different light shone on the root cause of my estrangement from the family. Could it really be true Louie wasn't my biological father? Did my mother keep that potent fact from me, even during the many years we'd spent together after our reconciliation? A tiny part of me still clung to the hope none of it was true.

Chapter 3

The first thing I did when I woke up the next morning was phone my cousin Inara, my mother's niece. I thought her a more reliable source than my paternal cousins.

"Louie was not your father, your actual father," was her answer to my question. "I feel terrible telling you on the phone like this. I was sure you must have known by now, sure your mother must have told you after all these years. Everybody on both sides of your family knew that Louie was not your father and we all wanted Ludy and Louie to tell you. But they didn't want you to know."

"Why?" I asked.

"The stigma of being an unwed mother in the 1950's, I'd guess. Why she didn't tell you when you got older is anyone's guess."

"Do you think she got pregnant in Europe before emigrating to the U.S.?" I asked.

"No. I remember hearing the guy was a sailor from upstate New York. Ludy's mother Natalia was very against the relationship."

"Why?"

"I don't know exactly why. But Ludy had you out of wedlock and that was very shameful to your grandmother. My mother and I went to the hospital to see Natalia when she was ill. I was 12 at the time. Remember, she wasn't my mother's mother." Ludy and Tessie had different mothers, a fact I had only learned in the last year or so.

"Ludy had just starting dating Louie at that time," Inara continued. "Your grandmother was discharged from the hospital, and she collapsed and died in the hospital elevator. I met you a short while after that. You were about three."

I have a photo of Inara, her brother Andrew and me on the front porch steps of my Aunt Tessie's brick home on Long Island, New York. I was sitting between my two cousins. It's the first photo I have of us together. I look about 3 years old. I asked Inara why we hadn't met before then and she told of a family rift, healed only after my mother's mom died.

"Was my real father Jewish, like Louie?"

"No, definitely not Jewish," she said. "You're not Jewish."

"Did my father know about me? Did I know him?" I asked.

"I don't remember. I'm so sorry. I just don't know," Inara said. She kept repeating how sorry she was as we hung up the phone.

*

For hours, I was in shock. Shaking, staring into space. Crying. Angry. Sad. So sad that I'd probably never know the full story of what happened. Why had my mother never told me? I realized that as far as I knew, there was no one alive who knew the details of what happened. Questions were all I had. How did my mother support us all when I was a baby? Her mother and me and herself? She always said she arrived in the United States with nothing, worked low-paying jobs. Did my real father know about me? And that swing in the doorway of an apartment I seemed to remember...whose apartment was that? Was that before Louie came into the picture?

Searching for clues, I got out old photo albums. There was a studio quality sepia 8 X 11 portrait of chubby-faced me as a baby sitting on my mother's lap, a shy, toothy smile on her lips, her widow's peak prominent. Several black-and-whites of just me; in one I'm in a baby carriage; in another, smelling flowers. In one, my mother, in a stylish mid-calf winter coat, and me in leggings, dress-length coat and a hat, are posed by a lake, a swan swimming nearby. Our clothes are good quality. Where did the money for those clothes come from?

I look about three years old in the first photo I have of me and my father.

"He was always behind the camera," my mother explained when I asked her once why there were no earlier photos of us.

I'd always been puzzled by the air of estrangement in that photo. We're sitting on the grass, me next to the right side of his body. He's leaning back on outstretched arms, knees bent in front of him, argyle socks exposed under his hiked-up pants, looking off to the left, a distant gaze on his face. My face, bangs cut straight across my forehead, is scrunched up, not happy. There's no father/daughter fondness in our pose, no adoration. No love.

I also found two faded black and white small photos of my father and me, maybe 5 now, on the deck of a ship. In one, I'm standing on a seat, our heads at the same height, both of his arms are around me, both of us staring straight ahead. Another 2 X 3 inch photo, bent and creased lengthwise, is of my father, in a white shirt and tie, seated behind a desk, typewriter in front of him, desk lamps aglow. "Warsaw Embassy 1952" written on the back in his scrawl. I had always assumed a mistaken date, but now I knew better. I was born in 1951, before he'd met my mother.

My hopes rose when I realized my birth certificate might shed light on the growing mystery. I dug into a file folder labeled "important papers", found the yellowed document with an official seal in one corner: Borough of Manhattan, New York, N.Y., Oct. 1, 1965. My birth date, November 13, 1951, is above the box for my mother, Ludmilla Podnick, and her "usual residence" of 464 East 115th St., NY. "Corrected Certificate Approved for Filing September 30, 1965" with a registrar's signature, is in a small box below the Father box, which lists Louis Ballin March as my father. On the bottom of the certificate is the disclaimer:

> "NOTICE: In issuing this transcript of the Record, the Department of Health of the City of New York does not certify to the truth of the statements made thereon, as no inquiry as to the facts has been provided by law."

"Oh, there was some kind of glitch in the system and we had to get your birth certificate reissued," answered my mother when I'd asked her years ago about the issue date of 1965, fourteen years after I was born.

Some glitch! I was furious when I realized the magnitude of my mother's cover-up, her outright lie. How in the world did she get my real birth certificate changed? And what happened to my original one? Energized, I was hopeful that researching the New York vital statistics archives would produce my original birth certificate with my biological father's name. Disappointment sucked the air from my lungs when my NYC.gov internet chat partner relayed the news that the state of New York destroyed my original birth certificate when the corrected one was issued. They cannot provide the original. Had my birth father's name been wiped from history?

Misericordia Hospital, where I was born, seemed a strange name for a hospital. My mother had mentioned it was a Catholic hospital, run by nuns. I wished I'd been more curious when she was alive, researched its history. Returning to my laptop, I found that Misericordia hospital was a hospital for poor and unwed mothers run by the Sisters of Misericorde, a Catholic order started in the mid-1800s in Canada. The sisters came to New York City in 1887, and the following year opened the New York Mothers' Home of the Sisters of Misericordia. They later purchased a large house at 531 E. 86th St., where I was born. A Wikipedia article states:

> "The order was particularly sensitive to the social stigma attached to a woman who had born an illegitimate child. The

sisters perceived that, by precluding other employment, this often tended to force a woman into prostitution, and in some cases infanticide. The hospital was associated with a NY foundling home for children who had been abandoned and left for the public to find and save."

I collapsed in tears. I was an illegitimate child. I was not abandoned.

I imagined my mother was offered the option of giving me up for adoption, maybe even pressured to do so. She kept me. Another surge of emotion moved through me at this realization – gratitude? A recognition of how much she must have wanted me, how much she loved me? An acknowledgement of what a struggle she must have gone through to birth, keep and raise me in the early 1950s? My sister and I had often talked about her strength and resilience; how she managed to persevere and thrive in her life.

If Louie March wasn't my biological father, who was? I ordered DNA kits from both 23andMe and Ancestry.com, hoping to compare their results and search two data bases for relatives. What were my paternal roots? Who am I?

Chapter 4

"You and I have something in common," I said to Eli, my son, age thirty-one. He, Walter and I were seated around the dining room table, about to dig into our first meal together since my return from New York.

"Turns out I don't know who my biological father is." I relayed the story of discovering the lies about my paternal roots.

"What an eerie coincidence," Eli said. Usually a ravenous eater, his fork had hovered above his plate during my entire tale.

Eli didn't know who his biological father was either. My husband Walter and I, unable to conceive a child on our own, turned to artificial insemination with an anonymous sperm donor. Eli knew how he was conceived and had thus far chosen not to try to find his biological father.

Walter and I always knew we were going to tell Eli the truth about his origins. We'd debated about the right time to do so since he was a toddler. Would knowing shake his confidence, destroy his sense of being loved and wanted, or imperil his connection to the main male figure in his life? Each time we weighed the pros and cons, we'd decided to err on the side of waiting, waiting until we were confident he was secure in his sense of self. We waited until he was 21, thriving as a junior at the University of California, Santa Cruz. It was time he knew.

We were both petrified that after we told him our family would be forever destroyed. Walter was worried that Eli would stop thinking of him as his father, that he'd grow distant. I was a nervous wreck, sure that Eli would be furious that we had deceived him for years. I'd convinced myself he'd deem our relationship fraudulent, and reject us.

"We have something important to tell you," I said to Eli, who had come over for breakfast in the apartment Walter and I rented for a week in the idyllic California beach town near his college.

"That sounds serious," said Eli, leaning back in his seat.

"After dad and his first wife had two kids, Shawn and Tara, they decided they didn't want any more, so he had a vasectomy," I said. "Do you know what that is?"

"They cut something so the guy can't have any more kids." Eli squirmed in his chair.

"Yes, basically," Walter said. "And when your mom and I got together we really wanted to have a child, so I tried to get the vasectomy reversed. But the reversal only works in a small percentage of cases, and it didn't work for me."

"Oh," Eli drew out the word, a wave of concern rippling across his face.

"And we had to decide whether or not to give up our dream of having a baby or to use a sperm donor to get me pregnant," I looked into his eyes. "You are our dream baby."

"Who was the guy?" Eli asked, looking from one face to the other.

"We didn't know him," I said. "We went to a fertility doctor near Boston and chose from three different donors. All we know is that he was a medical student in the Boston area, of Eastern European decent, and he was tall and athletic."

"So I'm not Irish and Scottish?" Eli's shoulders slumped. "I'm not really from the Cameron clan?"

"I put you in the Cameron clan myself," Walter said. "You're part of me whether or not I'm actually your biological father. I wanted you the second your mother conceived you."

"I always really liked being part of that heritage," Eli smiled.

"You get to keep that if you want to," said Walter, his eyes tearing up. "You're my son, no matter what."

"We weren't sure when we should tell you this," I said. "Whether to tell you when you were little, or to wait. Obviously we decided to wait." I held my breath.

"I'm glad you didn't tell me before this," Eli said. "I don't think I would've understood it. It could be kind of confusing if I were younger."

"If you're saying that to keep us from feeling bad, you don't have to," I said, sweating now, my voice shaking. "We really want to know what you think, what you're feeling.

This is big stuff, and you are entitled to feel whatever you feel and we can handle whatever comes our way."

"I get it," Eli said. "But dad is the only dad I know. He's still my dad. The other guy is just, well, just not in the picture."

"There's no hurry to finish this conversation now," Walter stretched, exhaling a long breath. "We're in Santa Cruz for the whole week, plenty of time to be together, talk, have fun."

"Cool," Eli said. "Are there any more bagels?"

*

Now, ten years after finding out he was not Irish and Scottish on his father's side, Eli was being told his maternal roots were also unknown.

"So we're not part Jewish?" he said, looking at me across the dining room table, his eyes narrowed in concentration as he did the mental gymnastics to unravel the implications of my story.

"We'll know for sure when I get the DNA results," I said.

*

A few weeks after Walter and I told Eli the facts about his paternity and the sperm donor, I was driving my mother home and telling her how the conversation unfolded.

"Why did you tell him?" she said.

"The truth is always best," I said. "He had the right to know."

"What difference does it make?" she said. "Walter is his father."

"Eli could've found out some other way," I said. "Other people knew. You've always known. And besides, the medical history could be important. It was important to us that he know the truth."

My mother was uncharacteristically silent for the remainder of the trip.

This memory, coming after I awoke one morning weeks after returning from New York with the news about my father, felt like the sky opened up and spoke to me. My body remembered it, not my mind. Here was a perfect chance for my mother to tell me about my true origins. She and I both had a complicated story about our off-spring's paternity. She could have taken the opportunity to open up with me, share her truth, make us closer. Instead, she chose, again, to remain silent. Why was she so compelled to maintain the lie?

Chapter 5

I waited, each day, for my DNA results to arrive. I waited to find out who I was now that I knew I wasn't who I thought I was. How dare they not tell me about my birth history? I stomped and raged, paced from the kitchen to the bedrooms and back again. I had the right to know! Beneath the rage was deep sadness. Tears that sprang out of nowhere. A passing question from, say, my acupuncturist, "How are you today?" and I'd start to cry, try to form a sentence through my ragged breath, try to express my shock at the depth of my parents' deception. I'd try to pull myself together.

My muddled mind ruled my days, along with a lethargy that either paralyzed me or propelled me to frantically pull myself out of sinking too low. I made plans to travel, join a tour, take a hike, swim, organize a closet, buy a new car – and then I'd second guess all my decisions – anything not to succumb to the deep well of despair I was so afraid of slipping into. I'd been depressed before. I didn't want to feel that helplessness again.

"Unexpressed rage is a cause of depression," my husband reminded me. "Let it rip."

So I'd let myself rant. "Who the hell was this guy pretending to be my father? How dare they keep the truth from me!"

Underneath all the rage I blamed myself. What was it about me, what flaw in me gave my parents cause to lie? If I were better adjusted, or more resilient, or happier in general, I'd breeze through this new chapter in my life. It's not really such a big deal after all, is it?

"Sounds like a trap," a good friend opined. "You were a bad person, and that made it okay for your parents to lie. And now you're bad because you're upset they lied. Aren't you being just a bit hard on yourself?"

*

Along with the waiting and emotional upheaval came memories, memories of my childhood, memories of time spent with my mother, memories of who I was before finding out I wasn't who I thought I was. They'd come unbidden, when I was in the shower or swimming laps at the Y or upon waking up in the morning.

"I'm going to New York for a few weeks," my mother's words came to me one morning as I was brewing a cup of green tea. We lived in Lantana, Florida then and I was in junior high school. She'd said I'd have to stay with her friend Winnie while she was away. "Dad can't take care of you while he's working swing shift."

"Why are you going now?" I asked. "Why can't you wait until we can all go?" My mother had never taken a trip on her own before. We had taken many family summer road trips from Florida up to New York to see family.

"I just want to see my sister. I'm taking Vicki with me."

"But why now?" I persisted. "I want to go too."

"Just because. You'll be fine. Stop whining."

A few days before that my mother had thrown down my report card in disgust.

"A "C" in math," she'd spat out the words. Math had been her favorite subject in school and she prided herself on her ability with numbers, seemed to take as a personal affront my love of reading over arithmetic. She'd insisted I take an advanced math class, much to my protestations.

"You're hopeless," she'd pronounce as I struggled with the difficult theoretical math problems at the kitchen table, her mouth hardening into a thin line. "Why couldn't you have inherited my brain?"

I knew I was a disappointment to her. And now she was so disgusted with my "C" that she was leaving me.

The memory tugged at my mind. I got out my birth certificate again. "Corrected certificate approved for filing 9/30/1965." Was 1965 the year I was in that math class? Is that when she went to New York? I did the calculations. They added up. My parents must have known I'd need a social security card soon so I could get a summer job. The "glitch in the system" had to be fixed.

*

Walter and I and our four-month- old baby boy boarded a plane at Logan Airport in Boston on a bitter cold winter morning. Glad to leave down jackets, scarves and snowsuits behind, we flew down to West Palm Beach to celebrate the holiday with my parents.

I'd left my hometown as a young woman of 18, eager to escape the atmosphere of unmet expectations and anxiety I felt around my parents. Visits home were obligatory, never events I looked forward to. But this time, at 35 years old, I had the grandbaby I knew my mother had been waiting for, and I hoped the time would pass in the glow of excitement over a new baby, not to mention the general havoc that a tiny human being somehow manages to generate.

My mother's eyes gleamed with joy when she reached out for Eli at the arrival terminal, her face softening into smiles, her voice thick with emotion. Eli reached right back for her, all chubby arms and legs, a grin stretched ear to ear. My father, reed thin, his Bermuda shorts cinched at the waist by a belt, stood back and surveyed the scene, hands in his pockets.

Their condo, usually immaculate and orderly, was cluttered with a wind-up baby swing, playpen, stroller and plastic baby tub. My mother buzzed with tales of the bargains she scored at the local second-hand stores. Lulled by her chatter, the swaying palm trees and salty air, I felt myself relax.

Up early with the baby on Christmas Eve morning, the four of us sat around the table on the screened-in back porch. Warm and humid, the sun was already high and bright by 9 a.m. The air smelled faintly of fertilizer used to keep the lawns a bright neon green and the remnants of my mother's homemade cheese blintzes. Eli lay on my father's lap, his feet kicking like egg beaters at his stomach. The tan, spider web fine lines of my father's face, usually pulled taut over high jutting cheekbones, seemed to melt into a softer version of himself as he looked down at his grandson. Thinning salt and pepper hair framed his face in wisps of sideburns. Eli's bright blue eyes lit up as he grabbed his grandfather's index finger.

"He reminds me of my son at this age," my father said.

"What son?" I said. My younger sister was my only sibling.

"Louie," my mother barked his name, cut him a warning with her eyes.

"I had a son once," he said.

Stunned, I knew better than to flood him with questions, get emotional, risk the chance he'd clam up. I waited several seconds, said "Where was that?"

"I met a woman in New Orleans, one of my ports of call. She was a fundamentalist Christian." My father, as far as I knew, had always been a devout atheist. "We got married and she had a baby boy."

"When was this?" I asked.

"The mid 1930s," he said. "I was in my late twenties."

"What happened?" I asked, keeping my voice level.

"She cajoled me into attending a church service. There was one testimonial after another and then everybody started writhing around, speaking in tongues," he said, his tone flat, as if he were mulling over what to eat for dinner that night. "I stood up and shouted at the top of my lungs 'you're all a bunch of lunatics' and walked out. That was the end of the marriage. I left town."

"How old was your son then?" I choked out the question, almost whispered it, afraid any big reaction on my part would freeze his telling.

"Oh, around two," he answered after a pause to calculate the years in his head. "I never saw him again." As sure as credits roll at the end of a movie, his features shuffled to signal the end of the conversation; a sigh filled his ribcage and slipped out of pursed lips before they lengthened and clamped to a thin line; a shiny glaze swam over his eyes as his gaze sought the palmetto palms outside the screened-in porch. He handed Eli over to me, got up.

"Dad, wait," I said.

He picked up the empty plate in front of him, looked at me and without saying a word, walked into the kitchen where my mother had busied herself earlier.

I sat in silence. My husband stared at me, his jaw slack with disbelief, eyes full of concern. Questions flooded my mind. Why did he never see his son again? Why did he wait until now to tell me? Who was this man who could leave a son and never see him again? I had always admired him, convinced his aloofness came from an absent-minded dreaminess, a superior intelligence, a longing for more than his life had brought him. Now I was faced with cruel facts of a colder nature. I hugged my baby boy close. A brother! Somewhere I had a brother! Did he have my father's build, my nose, our love of books? Did he have a family? Could I find him?

*

Several months before my mother died, at 89 years old, she was at my house for lunch. I was telling her about a

Netflix comedy special about Jewish humor and how much I could relate to the jokes.

"It's a Jewish thing," I'd said. "I just get it."

"You're not Jewish," my mother said under her breath, half turned away from me, her slight frame stooped at the waist.

I ignored her comment, focused on setting the table for lunch, slicing the roasted beets, crumbling the goat cheese.

"I'm not Jewish," Louie had said time and time again when any mention was made of his heritage.

"Judaism is a religion, and I'm not religious, therefore I am not a Jew," he'd elaborate.

"This sociology notion that somehow Jews are a certain culture, or people, that's bullshit. Why would I claim being Jewish? Because my uncles lived in a shtetl in Poland?" his voice rose an octave. "You are not a product of your past. Those people have no claim on me." His words gathered steam, his lips moist now with spray from his mouth. "All their yarmilkes and payos, the bowing and scraping at the waist in prayer…to who? God? What God? Some mass delusion," he said, a steel glaze to his blue eyes. "Masses of asses," he'd explode with a favorite phrase of his, often directed at any and all churchgoers. "I want nothing to do with all that nonsense."

So when my mother said "You are not Jewish" I assumed she was repeating my father's mantra about religion. My mother, raised Catholic, was just as dogmatic in her atheism as my father. I didn't want to get into an argument with her before sitting down to eat. I said nothing, as I often did to avoid friction between us. I'll never know, had I pressed the point, whether she would've told me the truth of my paternity that day. I imagine she must have contemplated telling me. Did the weight of her deception keep her awake at night?

Losing my Jewish heritage hurt more than losing my biological connection to the man I thought was my father. I'd had 26 years to recover from being disowned, years to build an identity separate from one dependent on his reflection of me. After my father's damning letter, I changed my last name from March, my maiden name, which I'd retained well into my marriage, to Cameron, my husband and son's name. I never thought of, or called, my father "Dad" or "Father" anymore. "Louie" was how I thought of him.

But I'm not Jewish? Louie and his mother, my grandma Ida, were my Jewish roots. We didn't practice the Jewish religion, any religion, but I was raised with matzo ball soup and gefilte fish; shmendrik, oy vey, mishegas – Yiddish is embedded in my vocabulary. In recent years I had come to value the cultural aspects of Judaism, the love of knowledge and Tikkun Olam, repair the world; believed they are transmitted from generation to generation regardless of religious belief.

My Grandma Ida escaped Poland and Jewish persecution in the early 1900's; she snuck across the border into Germany on a wagon under a load of hay, made her way across land and ocean to the lower east side of Manhattan. My Polish great uncles, revolutionaries, had been killed before WWII began. All their relatives, from a tiny shtetl near Warsaw, had perished. I admired my Grandma Ida's chutzpah and the revolutionary ideals of my great uncles. I treasured my half-Jewish roots. Now I'm told they are not my roots.

Who am I if not Jewish?

*

My mother and I were watching my son Eli, two-and-a-half years old, devour his lunch. Eli, chubby-cheeked and all smiles, was seated in his highchair, the white plastic tray strewn with bite-size pieces of tofu, avocado and sliced peaches.

"When you were a kid you just stopped swallowing your food," my mother turned to me and said. "I'd see this lump under your upper lip," she screwed her face up, lodged her tongue under the left side of her top lip, pulsed it in and out. "You'd chew it to a pulp, but refuse to swallow." Her words slurred around her pulsating tongue.

"When was that?" I asked. "How old was I?"

"Oh, around three," my mother said.

"Three?" I repeated, puzzled. "I must have been eating solid food by then, right?"

"Of course," my mother snorted. "That's what I'm telling you here. You'd been eating like a normal kid and then one day you stopped chewing and swallowing your food." Her voice rose in exasperation. "Well, you'd chew it a little, then shove a wad of it under your lip."

"Why do you think I did that?" I probed. The early childhood development classes I'd taken for my job in pediatric physical therapy had taught me kids didn't just stop eating for no reason.

"Who the heck knows." My mother flapped her arms up, hands bent back in an "I give up" gesture. "Stubborn. You always were stubborn. And too sensitive for your own good."

"More, mommy, more," Eli kicked his feet against the highchair footrest.

I stood up, walked over to the kitchen counter to cut up more avocado and tofu. Stubborn. Not the first time I'd been accused of that.

"So what did you do?" I swallowed the rising bile in my throat. Don't react, I told myself. Just try to get the facts.

"Louie came up with the idea of putting a whole meal in the blender," she said, coming over to stand next to me near the cutting board. "Everything went in – meat, potatoes, even salad. We'd grind it to a pulp. It came out looking like a greyish-brown mash. We'd sit you in the high chair, strap you in and shovel it into you." She grinned a rigid smile, looked me square in the eye, her voice triumphant.

"How did that go?" I asked, lowering my eyes to the cutting board.

"You didn't like it at first. But you had to swallow it. The mush wouldn't stay under your lip. The whole migillah went on for months, the blending. But eventually you went back to normal."

I had a dozen more questions but knew better than to raise her ire by casting doubts on her child-raising practices. I swallowed my repulsion at her story and turned back to my smiling baby boy.

That evening at dinner Eli patiently practiced piercing his pasta and vegetables with a fork. "All gone, mommy," he announced after he'd picked up the plate and licked it clean. I didn't have an appetite and mostly just pushed my meal from one side of the plate to the other.

What would have to happen for Eli to suddenly resist eating, to stop swallowing his food? What had happened to me when I was three years old?

Later in the week I dreamt I was feeding Eli in his high chair. In the way that dreams do, his face became the face of a little girl with brown eyes and bowl-cut brown hair. Her face morphed and stretched and grimaced as she shook her head left and right, left and right. "No, no, no," she whimpered, her body writhing upwards, the restraint strap of the high chair cutting into her thigh, my thigh. Bang, bang, bang – her feet/my feet pounded the wooden footrests. "No, no, no," her voice/my voice rose to a yell. Clink, clink, clink – a metal spoon ricocheted off my teeth.

I, somehow an adult again in my dream, picked the girl-child up under her arms. Liquid shit, grey-brown and gelatinous, poured down her leg, an endless pouring, covering my arms, sticking to my torso, puddling up on the floor. She was slipping through my arms. "I'm losing her," I thought. I grabbed her tighter. "No, no, no," she shrieked. "I won't eat that."

I woke up, stunned, sweating.

I worked with a team of early-childhood specialists. Experience taught us that a young child's eating issues are often the child's attempt to gain control over her environment – to exert a semblance of power in a stressful situation in which she feels powerless and misunderstood.

What was happening in my home when I was three years old?

I don't consciously remember being strapped into a high chair, mushy, grey gruel shoveled (or do the words force-fed apply here?) down my throat. My mother told me it happened. I believed her. Where in my body was the memory secreted away?

"You're grinding down your teeth," my dentist explained as she fitted me for a night-guard to be worn during sleep.

"Try eliminating gluten, soy and dairy from your diet," a nutritionist advised me, trying to get to the bottom of my gut problems.

"Prozac won't work if you don't take it consistently," my therapist reminded me as we discussed my recurring depressions.

With my mother's latest revelation, I now had a clue to the origins of my adult maladies. The mystery of what had occurred in my childhood home to provoke my eating behavior still remained.

*

I was five years old and my parents and I were staying at the Cadillac Hotel, a seedier version of the art deco masterpieces further down Collins Ave., the main tourist drag in 1950's Miami Beach. Snowbirds from New York, we drove to Florida after my pediatrician diagnosed me with walking pneumonia and told my parents they had best take me out of the cold, damp Bronx winter for a couple of weeks. Even the air was different in Florida, warm and salty through my nostrils, visible as it waved the palm tree fronds through the sparkling blue sky and rode the tops of ocean waves in bursts of white foam spray.

We spent our first morning at the hotel pool, my parents in matching lounge chairs under an umbrella, me nearby on the first two steps leading to the shallow end of the pool. The hot sun burned the skin over the jutting bones of my exposed shoulders. I looked up to see a tall, thin man in a tight, tangerine swimsuit talking with my parents.

"I can teach any child to swim in thirty minutes or less, or your money back," the man said. My swimsuit straps cut into my flesh as I craned my neck to follow the adult conversation.

"Let's give him a try," said my father, his wet bathing suit clinging to his bony legs. "We're here for another week; she may as well learn to swim."

"Come here, Genie," said the man. His skin was shiny, his blond hair slicked back. He extended a hand in my direction.

"No." I stood up and I backed away from the outstretched hand. I wanted no part of him or the big blue rectangle of water that I couldn't see the bottom of. I knew how to swim just fine in my neighborhood pool back home, its tall stainless-steel fountain in the middle, water spraying down on me and my friends as we waded and splashed. Nothing like this big blue pit I stared at now, its glassy surface hiding secrets down below.

"Do it," my father commanded.

I was up, up in the smooth, warm arms of the man, up in his unfamiliar smell.

"No, down!" I squirmed and kicked.

He carried me to the end of the diving board and then I was out of his arms, suspended in the air for a few seconds. A shock of cold water rushed past me as I sank to the bottom of the pool, a whoosh of noise past my ears, bubbles foamed in front of my eyes, the weight of the water squeezed me inward. I rose to the top, not a second to spare, my cheeks bursting with held breath, arms flailing.

"Now swim to the edge of the pool," the man on the end of the diving board yelled. "Go ahead, you can do it."

Darkness as I closed my eyes and sunk down, then resisted the sinking, struggled and flailed, coughed and sputtered. I pushed and pushed, fought and kept going. I was at the edge of the pool, the concrete rough against my fingertips, my eyes burning, chest heaving. The man lifted me out of the water. "Put me down," I cried. I felt the hot concrete on my feet and a towel draped over my shoulders. What could I do to make sure I wouldn't be thrown in the water again?

My father walked over to the man and me.

"You're stupid," I said to my father. Instantly I knew I was in trouble.

"Apologize right now," he said. "Apologize for calling me stupid."

"No, I won't." I held on, fought for some kernel of myself in the pit of my stomach.

"Apologize or else."

"No."

"I'll give you one more chance to apologize to me or else you'll get locked in the hotel room and you'll stay there, alone, while your mother and I go to dinner."

Nausea rose in my throat. I knew the feeling of being locked away. I waivered. Do I want that darkness around me, that chill of aloneness? My angry little self rose up in defiance.

"No, I won't," I looked him right in the eye. A stony cold glare looked back at me.

My fate was sealed. My parents dressed for dinner. I was cast out of their circle of togetherness. They left me in our little room with the double bed and roll-a-way cot in the corner. The dead bolt clunked as they turned the key and their footsteps sounded down the hall.

They were really gone. I sat there in the corner between the door and wall, curled into myself, alone with a familiar feeling of shame. Something shifted inside me. I moved to lie on the floor in front of the door, my feet flat against the barrier to the outside world. I kicked, over and over and over again, cried and screamed. The door opened. A man in blue and white stripped coveralls brought me to the front desk. I waited as someone went to get my parents from the dining room. I had thwarted their plans. Kicking and screaming in the hotel room, not staying silent, gave me power. This revelation, a coiled worm in my gut, both elated and terrified me. What would my father do now?

*

Scenes from my past crowded my waking hours. The revelation about my paternity was a new frame for the puzzling, troubled undercurrents I'd always felt in my childhood home. For that, I was grateful.

Chapter 6

The seemingly interminable wait for my Ancestry.com DNA results gave me a lot of time to think about lying - the conscious act of deciding, year after year, decade after decade, to withhold facts that people around you, loved ones, might find vital. I'd heard it said that not telling isn't really lying. It's just not saying anything, withholding, which is different than passing untrue information through one's lips.

Webster's Unabridged Dictionary dispelled this notion, defining the verb lie as:

> 1. To utter a falsehood with an intention to deceive; also, to utter falsehoods habitually
> 2. To cause an incorrect impression; to present a misleading appearance

I thought a lot about the stories told about me as a child, the stories about how I lied from an early age, stories that were repeated many times, at dinner tables, to illuminate this flaw in my character.

"Don't know where she picked it up, the lying," my mother would start in with a glance at me. My six, eight, or eleven-year-old stomach, depending on the year of the telling, clenched. I knew what was about to be revealed. Around the dinner table, the adults, relatives or neighbors slouched in their seats, fingered wine glasses, the meal over but before the plates were cleared and the kids excused to go play. The pitch of my mother's voice rose. In my earliest transgression, I was three years old. We lived in an apartment on Walton Avenue in the Bronx, with a radiator in the kitchen and a green formica-top kitchen table and matching green padded cushions on the chairs. I stood accused of taking a banana from the fruit bowl on that shiny green table without permission. Accused of eating said banana and stashing the tell-tale peel behind the radiator.

"The whole apartment smelled like rotten bananas," my mother recounted. "I went nuts, crawled around on the kitchen floor to find where the stink was coming from," she flailed her arms and legs to mimic crawling, always telling the tale with her comedic mix of hilarity and horror, eyes wide with disbelief. "When I got a yardstick to reach the black peel to pull it out from behind the radiator and showed it to you," she pointed her finger at me, "you refused to admit you put it there."

The adults in the room tittered, faces a mix of pity and plastered-on smiles, not sure how to respond. My father, rocking his chair on its back two legs, had a half-smile, half sneer on his lips. Skin ablaze, seething, I sat shame-faced, tight-lipped lest I show any emotion and crack in two.

If she were on a roll, my mother would follow with the story of green mucous that streamed copiously from my nose for a day or two when I was four years old.

"Worried, I took her to the pediatrician," my mother eyebrows knitted together with exaggerated concern. "He extricated a button lodged up high in her nasal cavity," her hands clasped above her head, mimicking a twisting, pulling motion, lips screwed up in concentration.

"You refused to admit you'd shoved it up there," my mother, again wide-eyed and mouth agape, shook her head at me. "Already so stubborn."

Suspect. Scrutinized. Othered. A rock turned over to discover the underside. Looking back, the feelings remain to this day. I can almost hear my parents and relatives in the know about my paternity whispering to each other "Who is she going to turn into, the one with those other genes?"

*

By the time I was nine years old my parents were convinced I was a compulsive liar. Not just a fibber, but a real liar. Fibs were harmless, like when the next-door neighbor called to invite Mom over for coffee and mom said, "No, I have a headache," but really she thought the woman was a bore because she sold Avon. Fibs were when Dad pocketed the seventy cents change the guy at Dairy Queen gave him back from his dollar for my forty-cent ice cream cone. We laughed at fibs, but I was a real liar. My parents said so.

I had a list of whoppers by the end of third grade. There was the time I insisted I heard a peeping Tom outside my bedroom window and sent my father traipsing, not once, but three times, into the night, flashlight in hand. My mother, standing at my doorway without my knowing, caught me, hand poised to rap on my window, my own intruder.

A month later me and the boy across the street got caught by his grandma in her laundry room with our pants down. I denied ever being there.

"The final straw," according to my father, was when I came home from school holding my throat, soundlessly mouthing the words "I can't talk." My mother, worried, called the doctor. He told her to hold my head over a pot of boiling water so the steam would open up my bronchioles.

"Ouch, it's too hot," I said aloud before I realized I was giving up my game.

This time they were going to cure me of my lying heart, once and for all. I was banished to my room for the entire weekend.

"You just sit there and think about what you've done," my mother commanded, veins bulging at her neck. "Why do you do this to me?" she asked, eyes ablaze.

I really didn't know. I didn't know what made me want a peeping Tom of my own, why I wanted to be voiceless for an afternoon. A hair of an idea would come to me and in a snap of time, before I could reason it out, contemplate the consequence, I'd be in the middle of my own home movie, caught up in the momentum, not knowing how to stop or why I was continuing. But my parents knew. "She craves attention, any kind of attention," my father said. My mother nodded her agreement. I knew wanting attention was a bad thing. It meant I was selfish. A bad daughter.

During my weekend punishment for mimicking a lost voice, I sat in my room, white walls broken only by the oval mirror over a low dresser my mother bought at a model home sale, one complete wall of jalousie windows framed by hospital green curtains. It was neat and clean and smelled of Murphy's oil. That morning, like every Saturday morning, I had dusted and vacuumed. The blue and green flowered bedspread had a sharp crease enfolding the pillows. The small wooden desk was bare on top except for a desk blotter and lamp in the corner. There was absolutely nothing to do in this room.

I really was sorry. I wished I could go back a couple of nights to when we'd all lie on my parent's bed, really two twin beds pushed together so you'd have to be careful not to fall into the crack, watching TV, Mom and Dad the bookends, my sister and I wedged between them, all cuddled together. During commercials my father would make hand shadow puppets on the wall, floppy bunny ears or gaping fish mouths, or show us how to do "here's the church, here's the steeple, open the door and here's all the people" with his long, bony fingers.

My mother had soft doe eyes on nights like that. She wanted to hold my hand as we lay side by side watching the Ed Sullivan Show. She wasn't like my friend's mothers. People were always asking her where she was from; they said she had a foreign accent. I only heard the way she'd mix up her v and w, saying "vindow," for "window," "vater" for "water." She had been a model and wore big white pearl sunglasses, slim fit dresses belted with wide white leather. She was beautiful, fragile, with bird-bone thin wrists, a perfectly straight nose. Even when sitting still she buzzed with energy, like a cat about to pounce on a bird, only a slight flick of its tail revealing excitement. She liked to go out, to have plans; she had opinions on world affairs, liked opera. I was sure my childish needs bored her; our tract home in the languid heat of the south Florida suburbs was a disappointment.

Lying on my bed, mulling over options for amusement during my captivity, I heard rustlings at my door, noise in the hallway and thought maybe my mother had had a change of heart.

"We're leaving. You stay where you are," my father said through my window, his words tight, gruff. Three car doors slammed.

I knew the doorknob locked on my side of the door so they couldn't really lock me in. I could escape as soon as their car drove away.

But that's not what happened.

When I pulled at the door it only opened an inch or two. Puzzled, I pushed my body flat against the wall, crammed my head into the corner so I could position one eye to look out the crack. I saw a rope suspended in the hallway. They must have tied the rope from my doorknob to the doorknob of the closed bathroom door across the hall.

I shouldered my weight into the door, but it didn't budge. The tick of my bedroom clock filled the room, my eyes traced the shimmer of dust particles caught in a shaft of mid-afternoon sun. Trapped, alone. The walls of the room moved in closer, the sunlight faded.

An ocean of fear pulled me into its undertow, swirling, the shore receding, any hope of touching warm sand or warm arms impossible.

"Bad. Selfish. Liar," my parents' words repeated in my head.

I sat on the floor, curled up in a ball, ankles crossed, arms wrapped around my knees, rocking and banging my head into the frame of my bed and began to cry, sobs exhaled with each crash of my head. Trembling arose from so deep it vibrated my gooseflesh to attention, every hair on my body alert, my knees slick with snot and tears.

My bowels loosened. Panic gripped me. I rummaged through the bottom shelves of my closet and at the very back found a wide-mouth jar full of my mother's old buttons. I opened the jar and dumped the buttons onto my bed, recognizing one from my mother's red wool sweater, one from my sister's lederhosen, all from good days that would surely never come again.

Removing my shorts and underpants, I squatted over the jar, reaching behind me with one hand to squeeze my buttocks shut as I peed first, then relieved my clenched intestines. The walls watched me, the flowers on the bedspread eyes now, disgusted at my act. The trees, swaying in their outside freedom, knew of my degradation and told the birds and soon the world would be whispering my shame. Palms slick with sweat, I screwed the lid on the jar, wiped myself with my underpants and ferreted them both in the closet.

The room was full of the stench of my transgressions. Pulling the chair from under my desk I wedged my body up into the small space, the pressure of the wood pressing the skin onto my bones, holding in my blood and organs, keeping them from leaking out my wounded soul. I fell asleep.

I swam through the sea of their disapproval for days afterward. I'd walk by the kitchen and my mother would pause, knife in mid-air, to look at me, her mouth pursed, eyes narrowed, a sigh escaping from her expanded ribcage. My father stopped reading the newspaper, peered at me over his glasses, tapped his foot. Not talking to me, they exchanged meaningful glances at the dinner table.

Out in the world again, the walls of my room continued to press on me, an invisible confinement. I learned to test the electric charge of the air before acting, to shape my oscillations to join the existing wave of current. I wasn't going to take any more chances.

*

Now, seen through the lens of truth about my paternity, I imagine my childhood self was unconsciously acting out the undercurrent of secrecy and lies swirling around my home. Lying may well have been a means of getting attention. It certainly gave my parents the ammunition to point a damning finger at me, while they were the master perpetrators of deception themselves.

Chapter 7

Four weeks after spitting into vials and sending my DNA off for genetic testing I got some answers: 47.9% Eastern European, 38.0% Italian, 6.4% Greek/Balkan. I'm part Italian! My father was Italian!

"Italian!" my husband crowed. His mother was Italian. "No wonder I was instantly attracted to you!"

Italian explained my olive skin.

"You'd always get so dark every summer," my mother would say. "We'd all burn and peel, but not you."

Italian might explain my given name, Regina, which means "queen" in Latin and Italian. Uncomfortable with the upper-class connotations of the name, I'd shortened it to Gina in my teens. Did my birth father have a hand in naming me?

I debated whether or not to try and find him. I was 66 years old. Would my life change in any way if I knew who he was? Logic told me I'd still be the same person, still me.

Genetics didn't matter. My heart insisted that I find my Italian family and get to know those roots.

I lasered my focus on the DNA matches on my Ancestry.com site. Top on the list was Linda D., a possible 1st cousin. On June 5, 2018 I sent her the following message on the internal Ancestry site:

> Hi, I recently got my DNA results and you came up as a "high probability" 1st cousin. I found out last month from relatives that the father who raised me was not my biological father and I am interested in finding out the ethnicity and life story of my bio father. He would have known my mother in 1951 in New York City or nearby, when she was 25 years old and a recent immigrant from Europe. My ancestry composition results are mostly Eastern European and Italian. If anyone in your family has any information, I would be very appreciative. Thank you.

I sent a similar query to several other people listed as possible 2nd-5th- cousins on the Ancestry or 23andMe sites. Then I waited. I tried to make heads or tails out of the genetic information provided on the Ancestry site: Shared DNA (with Linda D.): 679 cM across 31 segments. What in the world did that mean? And how could it help me find my father?

Chapter 8

I was eighteen, living at home with my parents and sister, attending the local community college. A psychology major, I was failing a stenography class I started with the hope I'd be able to land a secretarial job. I needed a parent's signature to drop the class before the F would become a permanent stain on my transcripts.

"Ask your father," my mother said.

"What are you going to study instead?" my father asked. "That psychology nonsense? Hocus pocus, that's all psychology is, smoke and mirrors, dredging up old stories, inventing memories. It's hogwash. A pseudo-science. You're better off sticking with a real skill like stenography."

"I know that's what you think." It wasn't the first time I'd heard his disdain for the subject that had fascinated me since high school. In the late 1960's, interpersonal psychology was all the rage, and professors encouraged us to delve into our feelings toward others, to uncover the motivation behind our actions. During lectures about

Gestalt therapy, we were asked to sit knee-to-knee with another student, pretend the co-student was a person we had a conflict with, and tell that person how we felt, hold nothing back. Our classroom moved to a gym for lectures on primal scream therapy, and here we were encouraged to pound out our anger on thick mats. My classes helped me make sense of the complicated feelings I felt about my parents, the new knowledge a lifeline to a self where I might let go of feeling bad about myself.

"Just sign my form," I flapped the papers in front of him.

"I won't," he said, his lips in a tight, flat line. "I already told you, you're better off learning a real skill that'll get you a job."

"I'm old enough to make up my own mind. You can't tell me what to do." I raised my voice.

"Oh, yeah?" he countered. "Get out. How dare you talk to me like that?" He lifted his right elbow to shoulder height, hinged his forearm to and fro, repeatedly pointing his index finger toward the front door. "Get out of my house. Get out and don't come back."

My mother, at the stove in the kitchen, her head turned away from us, didn't say a word.

Shocked, I drove away with only my purse and the keys to my '63 Dodge Dart. I hadn't expected the escalation, the hardness of his stance. A familiar sense of confusion added to my anger and hurt. Was my behavior so horrible to warrant being kicked out of the house? At eighteen, I was a responsible teenager, did my household chores, got good grades, had a job to pay for my incidental expenses, didn't get in any trouble. Why had my request engendered such wrath in my father? What was it he had against psychology? What was it he had against me?

I drove to a place I knew I'd find camaraderie, the pier at Lake Worth beach, a local hang-out for my new college friends. Pulling into the parking lot, filled with cars with surf boards atop their roofs, I spotted a few familiar faces amid the mostly young crowd.

"Hey, what's happening?" Bobby said as he approached my car. Bobby's red hair, cut in a bowl-cut, framed the perpetual smile on his chubby freckled face. "I want you to meet some new friends from Key West." Happy, a Harpo Marx double and Bobby's side-kick, loped up behind him, blond curls bouncing around his ears.

Bobby and Happy led me to a madras bedspread on a sandy berm overlooking the shore and the pier. "Hey, man, join the good vibes," their friend said and moved over to make room for us to sit down.

How is it that teenagers bond with so little shared history, so little introduction, so little preamble? A nod of the head, a fringed jacket, a flash of a wine bottle – that's all we needed back then; a like soul, a harbor of acceptance, a refuge from judgement. That's what I longed for. So when my new friend passed the wine bottle, I threw my head back and drank deep.

The shadows of the palm trees had lengthened on the sand when the voices around me began to sound like cartoon characters. Soon neon pink and yellow swirled in the deepening blue of the waves, sparklers shimmered and exploded from the pier, which seemed to have unmoored from land, floating farther out to sea. Black velvet cloth, heavy like stage curtains, fell in front of my face, behind me, blocking me in. I was frightened, gasping for air.

Bobby and Happy noticed my distress, took me to their apartment. Palm tree fronds whipped and dipped low to the ground outside their second story window as the sky lit with streaking comets. My father's sneering face, orange-yellow like a harvest moon, bounced in the sky, visible even if I closed my eyes.

"A bad trip," Bobby said the next morning. "You tried to pry off the window screens, wanted to sit on the sill. We were afraid you'd jump out."

"Must have been some bad LSD," Happy chimed in. "Those guys must've put it in the cheap wine. Sorry. We didn't know."

*

A few days later, having found a roommate and an apartment, I returned home to pick up my clothes and other belongings. Almost finished packing up my car, I turned back towards the house to find my mother standing on the walkway, a cardboard box in her arms.

"Take this," she said, her eyes downcast. She thrust the box towards me. "A few old things from the house. Kitchen stuff, towels. You might need them." Her words were hesitant, her voice shaky. She looked up at me, her face drawn, the lines around her eyes and mouth furrowed. Was her box of material goods a peace offering? Did she disagree with my father's dictate?

"Thanks," I said, not trusting myself to say more, afraid I'd start to cry. I put the box on the passenger seat and drove away.

Chapter 9

A few weeks after I found out my biological father had Italian heritage, a guy with the name of cottonmike5 responded to my Ancestry.com query. Ancestry pegged us as third to fifth cousins. Mike said he'd ask others in his family what they knew. Hope sparked, then sputtered when a week later he reported he'd hit a dead end.

I felt a constant sense of dislocation. Just moving my leg through space felt other-worldly, in time-warp speed. Whose leg was I moving, after all? I used to think my body belonged to me, to the genetic history I'd assumed was mine. But now? Whose history was in my leg? How could I move through the days with the same cadence to my step? Did others sense my body was different now? Of course, I wasn't really different. Nothing had changed. I was still the same me. Wasn't I? My neighbors, even my immediate family, they all went about their days as if nothing had changed. Didn't they notice the earth had tilted?

I awoke one morning, swimming through the marsh reeds of a dream. *She was raped,* was my first conscious thought. *Of course, that's what happened. My mother was raped. I'm the product of that rape. No wonder she didn't want to tell me.*

I lay pinned to the bed by the weight of my deduction, terrified I was right. Was my biological father a rapist? Memories about my mother and times we'd broached the topic of sex flooded my mind.

"Down there," my mother would say to refer to my pubic area when I was a child. She'd nod her head strategically, eyes level, not a direct look at my 'down there', only a hint.

The boy next door and I were eight years old and one day we had the idea to see what the other had "down there". I ran to the laundry room in the back of my house, unzipped the zipper in the back of my gingham shorts, stepped out of them, turned them around and stepped back into them, with the zipper in front. Our rendezvous point was the driveway in front of the boy's house, behind a car. We sat on the blacktop, still warm in the wanning afternoon sun. My shorts were zipped down in front. I leaned forward to peer at his "down there".

"Lower," he said, reaching for my shorts. "I can't see anything." A shadow fell over his body. I looked up.

"What are you two doing?" my mother said. I don't remember what happened immediately after that. I do remember the scalding hot bath, the black and white square tiles in the bathroom.

"Clean yourself," my mother said, standing over me as I sat in the tub. "Down there. Scrub hard, or I'll do it for you."

*

When I was sixteen, about to step out the door of our house to meet the boy taking me on my first date, my mother tapped me on the shoulder.

"You know what *not* to do, don't you?" she said, nodding her head with significance, her eyes locked onto mine, lips pinched.

"Yes, Mom." I knew exactly what she meant, though we'd never talked about sex.

*

My new husband Walter and I, in my early 30's, were visiting my parents in Florida. My mother had invited a couple over for dinner, and the men were outside admiring the enormous mangos on my father's prize tree. My mother, her friend Winnie and I were in the living room, drinking wine.

The three of us are all married women, I thought to myself. I had proven I could be independent, succeed at marriage. Both my parents approved of Walter. Was it possible I could open up a little around my mother? Show my true self? I'd always longed for the type of closeness I'd read about in memoirs and novels. Mothers and daughters who were each other's closest confidants, whose love and admiration for each other were never in doubt, even when hashing out disagreements. I envied daughters who credited their sense of positive self- worth as a reflection of their mother's steadfast support and encouragement. I longed for that type of mother. Was this dinner party an offering of camaraderie? Perhaps I could risk letting go of my usual guard, testing of the emotional waters, and just say what was on my mind.

"Married sex, might be the best yet" I said, feigning a knowing air, my face rigid in a cloying smile, my body stiff.

"What's so good about it?" my mother snapped back at me archly, seemed to catch herself, turned and walked out of the room. I felt as if I had been slapped. Put back in my place. A chasm of dead space remained between Winnie and me. Why had I, out of the blue, made such a ridiculous comment?

Decades later, alone in my bed, I still cringed at my gaffe. But now, worse than embarrassment, my memories cemented a fear that my mother suffered a traumatic sexual experience. Had she been raped? Is that the secret she carried? On second thought, hadn't my cousin Inara, when queried about my biological father, used the word relationship? I reached for my journal, read the entry after our phone conversation. "Your grandmother was against the relationship," she'd said. My confusion about the story behind my origins deepened. My questions were unending. All I had was conjecture.

Chapter 10

When I spit in those test tubes and sent them off for analysis, I added my DNA to the gene pool of over twenty million people who had taken an at-home ancestry test. The internet teemed with stories of revelations from those tests, new-found fathers, brothers and sisters, and ancestries revealed. People were connecting in chat rooms to compare notes and find solace. On the PBS show, "Finding Your Roots", celebrities discovered their ancestry. A friend of mine became a genealogy sleuth, delighted to ferret out the mysteries of the genetic code, and helped her husband, adopted at birth, find his birth parents. But to me, the TV shows, the explanations of how to understand the mathematics of genetic matching, all that information was just a dull roar, background noise, overwhelming and annoying. Still raw from my discovery, I didn't have the mental edge to become an amateur genealogist.

All I really wanted to do was move my body – walk, bike, or swim. Moving quelled the nausea I felt anytime my mind drifted to the discovery about my father, which was anytime I wasn't focused on a hiking trail or my swim stroke. Increasing my heart rate seemed to reduce the queasiness in my stomach, so exercise became a daily, or often, twice a day, routine as I waited for a reply from potential relatives, especially my first cousin, Linda D.

"Any word?" asked Eli, my thirty-one-year- old son, riding his bike into our garage, face glowing with sweat and the endorphin high that comes from a hard workout.

"Nothing," I replied. "Maybe my constant checking has jinxed it. I log onto my Ancestry.com site, oh, I don't know, seven or eight times a day to check my messages."

"Maybe she just doesn't use her site much," he said. "Some people have their sites managed by relatives."

"Where does that leave me?" I said. I usually try to keep upbeat and positive around my son, not burden him with my woes. Burdened with my mother's moods, her depressions, and her insistence that she was owed my attention and care, I took a different tack as a parent.

Maybe I had swung the pendulum a little too far in the opposite direction as mother to my son. I read once that what kids really wanted was to see their parents as happy, well-functioning adults living full lives. That's the me I wanted Eli to see. He was thirty-one now, though, and I hoped we were ready for a more peer-to-peer relationship. I let my full self show a little more now.

"Sorry, Mom," he said. "That sucks. I mean, what more can be said about the whole damn situation?" He helped me carry the sandwich fixings and drinks from the kitchen to the back patio, loading up his long arms from elbows to hands.

Nothing makes me happier than being with my son. Several of my friends have confessed the same sentiment, the same joy at the opportunity to spend time with their grown offspring.

"You light up when he walks into the house," my husband often marvels at the phenomena. The sight of my son seemed to spark an arc in my brain synapses, to release the first note in a well-known symphony, set off the whole score.

Did my mother love me with this ferocity?

*

I was in the sixth grade and had been taking accordion lessons from Mr. Brendolin for three years. I'd been playing polkas and waltzes at the local German club on Saturday nights and Mr. Brendolin thought me ready to compete statewide. I needed a dress for the competition and my mother wanted to make one especially for me.

I stood on the low coffee table in our living room in my special dress. My little sister played on the floor nearby, her Barbie and Ken and their doll clothes piled next to her. The tang of sweet and sour stuffed cabbage raisin sauce simmering on the stove filled the air.

My mother's mouth was full of straight pins, the pointy tips in her mouth, the bright orange, red, yellow, green and blue tiny balls jutting out from her pursed lips.

"Turn around," she mumbled.

I felt my mother's hands on my waist smoothing the sateen fabric, a rose-pink color, not a light pink, but the color of a rose that's been dampened by the morning dew. The fabric, slightly shiny with dusky overtones, had delicate interwoven threads that gave it a three-dimensional texture. I thought it was beautiful.

My mother stood back to survey her work, her head tilted to one side, her eyes soft. She reached for a yardstick and measured the distance from the floor to the bottom of my hem. An exacting seamstress, she was making sure the hem was straight and secure. Again, I felt her hands smooth the fabric around my waist.

"Lovely," she said, smiling. "The color really suits you."

At that moment, I felt the warmth of my mother's love. If only I could keep her happy, she might love me like this always.

Chapter 11

In a photo on my bedroom wall, my mother and I sit under the arch of a wishing well, its iron filigree laced with tiny roses. Our bodies are on opposite rims of the well and we're leaning into each other, arms encircling each other's backs, heads together. The photo is printed in black and white, the circular frame carved, ornate wood. We look so alike, our hair lines and cheekbones, the point of our chins. We look as if we'd always been smiling together, close and uncomplicated.

Taken after our nearly four-year estrangement, the picture represents the reintegration of our lives, the attempt at working through our troubled history.

*

I flew into the West Palm Beach airport on the night of a full moon, a few months after the death of my father. By the time I'd rented a car and arrived at the Howard Johnson's motel on A1A, the moon, an orange orb, was etched with the greys of her caverns and crevices. The balmy air smelled like the years of my childhood spent here, on Lake Worth Beach - ocean spray, rotting seaweed, an undercurrent of french fries and double-mint ice cream. I stood at the entrance to my room, beseeching the moon to soothe my anxiety. She rhythmically pulled tides across our planet and affected humanity's core physiology. Perhaps she would lend her certainty of mission to my journey to retrieve my mother. I bade her calming presence goodnight and locked the deadbolt to my temporary home.

The pain I felt as a result of my mother's complicity with Louie and my banishment paled in comparison to the push I felt for connection with her. I didn't welcome the push, it was just there, an immutable presence, a constant gnawing at my insides, a gale at my back. It seemed primeval, the need for connection with one's mother, and rivaled a force of nature, like water seeking its lowest level or gravity's pull on wayward objects. I'd rather go through the fire I knew was awaiting me at her front door then bear the anguish of our separation any longer.

The next morning, after a fitful night's sleep, I made my way to my mother's condo. Needing to ground myself in the physical presence of the landscape before launching into unknown emotional terrain, I stopped first at Lake Worth Beach, rode through the parking lot toward the old pier. It was the end of summer, the south Florida sky bleached by the relentless heat, the air thick with humidity. I parked, walked out onto the pier, the wood planks splintered and cracked, the metal handrails rusty and peeling. A few fishermen sat on aluminum folding chairs tending their poles, white plastic buckets at their sides. Judging by the smell of bacon, my old high school hang-out, a café perched at the end of the pier, was still cranking out greasy fare. Now its welcome sign hung off-kilter and photos of triumphant fisherman posing with dead sharks, tacked on a bulletin board, were crinkled up at the corners, their color so faded I could barely discern people from fish.

The complex of three pools nearby where I'd learned to swim as a child was boarded up, piles of twisted plastic bags among the detritus swept against the plywood. Only the tourist shop was open now, conch shells in rattan baskets out front, snorkels and speedo swim suits, all looking washed-out by the sun, hanging in the window. Ahead was an open-air thatched pavilion, the scene of a Fourth of July party the summer between my junior and senior years of high school. Along with sparklers and banana splits from HoJos across the street, there was the drama of a girlfriend and I vying for the same boy. He chose me and the friendship with my girlfriend was never the same.

I rode south on the familiar beach route, my car windows rolled down, the taste of salt crusty on my lips. High-rise condos blocked the ocean view to the east, occasionally an opening, a peek of emerald-green blue water blending into the horizon. To the west the neon green of south Florida blared - grass, standing cypress, swaying palm fronds, variations of green broken by bursts of magenta bougainvillea. Languid, that's what a Florida late summer is, slow and dreamy. My limbs felt heavy, like I was pushing through thick cream. The weight of the air, the weight of my journey – I hoped I could push through.

I stopped at Delray Beach, kicked off my flip-flops, felt my toes sink into thicker than plush carpet grass on the berm overlooking the ocean. A memory of Louie surfaced. A low swag chain fence bordered the hedges on the bluff above the shoreline and my father, clad only in plaid Bermuda shorts, squatted in front of the fence, aping an organ-grinder monkey chained to a thick link of the fence. He contorted his bony arms, proffered a cupped, beggar's hand, and morphed his face into a pathetic grimace, cowed and miserable, gargoyle like. My mother, sister and I laughed at his antics while I, in my early twenties at the time, secretly wondered at his strange sense of humor. And now, decades later, I was still mystified by his motives and the cruelty behind his statement "you've been a thorn in my side since you were three." I choked down the lump welling at the back of my throat and brushed away my tears. My father was dead. And my mother awaited me.

Turning inland for a couple of miles, I entered my mother's condo development, Bent Tree Villas East, one of the ubiquitous housing tracts in southern Florida at the time and my parents' abode since moving from the home I'd grown up in a dozen years before. My mother called their home, a two-bedroom, one story condo attached by a garage to the next-door neighbor's garage, her "villa". Years before, long before Eli was born, when my parents first moved in, we all made a home movie, "Condo News", spoofing the homogenized nature of the housing tract. All the houses were the same beige paint, their landscaping identical as no original design was allowed by the homeowners association. All residents walking the manicured streets at dusk, were white, over 55. My sister's husband, a children's TV show writer, penned the script and Walter, an amateur film-maker, worked the camera. Louie, in a vest and sports coat, his wavy salt-and-pepper hair slicked back, played Horace Nit-pic, the chairman of the rules committee. "If you're having fun, you're doing something wrong," he dead-panned. Clad in a Tampa Bay t-shirt and straw hat, my mother gave the sports report, feigning a southern drawl and waving goodbye with a tennis racket.

The six of us had a lot of laughs together and the weekend stood out in my mind as probably the most enjoyable and stress-free time in our family history. My parents' joie de vivre during those few days gave me a glimpse of who they were beneath the distress that usually drove their behavior, who they were as individuals with their own history and experiences, apart from being my parents. I knew a funny and world-wise woman lived somewhere inside in my mother. She was the one I longed to reconnect with. I hoped she might be present when I knocked on her door.

*

"Oh, Genie," my mother said, calling me by my childhood name. "It's you. You came." Almost four years had passed since I'd seen anyone in my family of origin, four years since my father's damning letter. My mother opened her condo door wide.

I stepped over the threshold, sweaty and shaky, my lower lip quivering. It was easier to take her into my arms than to look into her eyes, with all their potential accusations. We hugged, wordlessly. What was there to say after all? I could still wrap my arms around her slight build and almost touch my own shoulders with my hands. My fingertips grazed the familiar knobs of her spine, the edge of her scapula. Her scent, a faint citrusy musk, unchanged. My mother.

"Let me look at you," she said and took a step back. We were still standing in the doorway. Her hands held my shoulders, her arms outstretched, her look appraising. The old flame arose in my throat. Was I good enough? Would criticism come? Relief, I think, was on both our faces, relief our ordeal was over, mixed with, on mine at least, a veneer to buffer rejection. Her face seemed drawn, her cheeks lined and sunken and her classic cheekbones jutted sharper than I remembered. Was that sadness in her eyes? She wore shorts that fell just above the knee, a coral cotton top. A forelock from her short-bobbed haircut curled onto one side of her forehead, a comma around her widow's peak.

I don't remember if I cried. I don't remember what we did after our initial embrace. My journal, too, is oddly absent of details.

Her condo looked the same, the cream-colored carpet, the wall of shelves with a crystal bowl filled with fruit carved from colorful stone, a few family photos, a wooden African statue of a figure, not clearly male or female. I felt as if I were in a museum I had frequented years before, checking for new acquisitions, relieved to find familiar touchstones, a remove to my interest, a distant appraisal.

We sat in the middle of her long, light blue sofa, turned toward each other, our knees, not quite touching, behind a coffee table made by my father years before. He'd inlaid four-by-four-inch decorative tiles depicting street scenes from Greece, Italy, and Morocco, purchased on their many overseas trips, on top of a crudely built wooden base to make the table. He was present in every angle of the wood, every choice of tile. I tried not to look.

I don't remember much of what we said during our first hour together, how we caught up on our estranged four years. I do remember my mother saying "I should have never let him send that letter". I felt a rush of fear at her direct reference, a fear of what might come next, and a flush of righteousness. *Damn right you should've nixed that letter*, I thought, relieved that she at least admitted some regret. Her comment about my father's letter was the only time during my two-day visit we spoke directly about what preceded our estrangement.

My breathing eased as time passed and our old familiar cadence resumed. We moved onto the small screened-in porch as the temperature cooled, the Mexican marble lamp still in one corner, a small TV on a shelf in the other. I showed her a few recent photos of Eli.

"Well," she said, her eyes darting away from the pictures. "He's grown." Pressure beat behind my eyes as tears welled up. *Is that all she's going to say about her grandson, my beautiful boy?* I thought. Anger bloomed hot on my chest. No, I chastened myself, don't go there.

"Don't expect too much," my therapist's words echoed in my head. "Your mother may not be capable of true intimacy. If reconciliation is what you want, you have to take her where she's at."

I knew that any plaintive note in my voice, anything less than delight with her behavior and actions had the potential to release a volcano of her anger and result in her turning the blame for the estrangement onto me. Hadn't she just said she wished she hadn't let Louie send the letter? I was amazed she'd admitted to even that. She'd never been one to apologize for anything, or show any capacity for self-reflection. She wasn't blaming me. She wasn't criticizing me. That in itself was an improvement. Maybe the blandness of her reaction to Eli's photo was her best possible reaction. At least we'd keep the peace.

Again, my therapist's voice filled my head. "You have to truly believe that you never deserved such harsh rejection from your family," she'd said. "You must know deep in your bone marrow that you are a good daughter, a good person. You can't depend on getting that message from your mother. You have to mother yourself."

I staunched my tears. Tried to breathe evenly. We both shifted in our seats. Then my mother fell into her gift of gab, chattered on about the Unitarian Universalist Fellowship she was a member of, the latest UU Women's Club she'd hosted in her home, what she served as appetizers, how every morsel had been eaten, where the latest circle dinner at the UU was held, the fancy home, the professors and lawyers in attendance. All I had to do was utter a well-placed 'oh, really?' and sit back and listen. That was the thing about my mother - she was a master of avoiding a deep dive into emotional terrain, or tackling the elephant in the room. She skated over the obvious with such ease, it was as if I were imagining the emotional upheaval of the last years. Was it all in my imagination? What was I so upset about, after all? We talked about recipes. She showed me a linen tablecloth and matching napkins she picked up for a song at the local thrift store. Did I only imagine the years of angst? Was I creating mountains out of molehills? Could it really be this easy to return to normalcy? Or was I dreaming, making all this up?

Why didn't I bring up the subject of our troubles myself? I liked to think I confronted issues in my life, dealt with problems. Why hadn't I insisted we talk it over? Partly, it was the advice from my therapist. And partly, it felt so familiar to assume this passive role, to let my mother run the show. I walked into her house and assumed a childlike role. I got what I knew I could get – we could have each other if we didn't really let down our guard, if we didn't really open up, if we just pretended. I didn't even consciously know the rules of our engagement. They came as if ether had been sprinkled on a daintily folded handkerchief and held to my nose and mouth. I was anesthetized into the old ways of being. I knew my place around her. I'd much rather endure the familiar ache of my younger years, the longing for a deep heart-to-heart connection with my mother, than risk an argument and a potential return to the fiery pain of our estrangement.

"There's a new restaurant I like," she said. "Let's go for dinner. It's close by."

She went into the master bedroom to change her clothes. I went to the bathroom in the hallway, the one with the blue and white wallpaper, sailing ships at sea, their masts aloft, an homage to Louie's seafaring days. My brown eyes stared back at me in the mirror. You're doing fine, I told myself.

As we entered the garage through the kitchen door, she pressed the garage door opener and the door rolled up. The floor was spotless, wall-to-wall white linoleum tile, even under the car. She saw me take it in.

"Louie did that," she said. "Put the tile down."

Louie. His presence everywhere except in our conversation.

"Nice," I swallowed the lump in my throat.

"Makes it easy to keep clean," she said.

*

Numb, I drove back to my motel that night. There had been no dramatic reunion scene, no teary declarations of love, no gnashing of teeth, no condemnations, no weepy confessions of remorse, no begging for forgiveness. That was good, right? That it was so easy?

Yet my hand shook as I fumbled to insert the key in my door. I stubbed my toe on the entry ledge and burst into sobs, my skin suddenly on fire, as if a two-ton metal plate had lifted off my body, releasing scalding steam, the roil below our seemingly easy reconciliation. The tumult of my emotions, suppressed all day, vented through me. At the end, I was left with sadness, sadness and confusion at my inability to be authentic with my mother. At her inability to be authentic with me. We were like two magnets held near each other with their positive poles pushing the other away. We'd get so close, yet not touch, a force field of quivering vibrations pushing us apart. We wanted each other. I knew we did. The desire was there. What was it that held us at a distance? I knew what kept me wary. I'd had years of flinching from her criticism and judgement. The force field of her whole being had always radiated a push outward, even when her words spoke differently. Her demeanor would soften and I would relax, expecting love, and instead, on a dime, she'd turn on me with a critical barb. I didn't want to risk it. I had enough work protecting my own fragile sense of okay-ness than to open myself up to her potential criticism and rejection. I knew what propelled the pole of my own magnet. What propelled my mother's? What was she protecting herself from? What was the reason for her armor? There must be a thread of logic that I could follow, a thread that would tug open a hidden portal, finally revealing the reason for our emotional disconnect.

My ruminations kept me awake throughout the night.

*

"Sleep well?" I asked my mother the next morning as she slipped into the passenger seat of my car. We had planned a walk in Palm Beach to pass the time.

"Like a log, like always," she smiled, lipstick smeared on one front tooth. "I lay my head on the pillow and the next thing I know the sun's shining through the blinds. You?"

"Pretty well," I lied, and waited for her banter to fill the silence.

We walked down Worth Avenue and then over to the gardens abutting the intercoastal waterway. Our strides fell into rhythm, my height only an inch taller than hers and our legs a similar length. She took my hand and I felt a swelling around her knuckles, a slight bend in her index finger at the tip.

"Arthritis," she said when I brought her hand up closer to my face to get a look. "Just like my mother. Let me see your hands." We put the palms of our right hands together, our fingers outstretched, their length, except for her bent index finger, identical, the oval of our nailbeds carbon copies of each other.

"You'll get it too," she said. "Arthritis. Just you wait and see."

My new Canon SLR camera hung from my left shoulder and bumped against my hip. I spotted a wishing well nestled against a backdrop of vivid green hedge.

"Sit here," I instructed as I brushed away the dead leaves around the perimeter of the well. Photography was one area I could be in control, take charge. I set the camera on a nearby wall, squinted through the viewfinder to set up the shot, palmed the remote shutter button and joined her on the lip of the well. We leaned toward each other, arms around each other's waist. My mother looked into my eyes, brushed her lips on mine. Her smile, the heat of the day, the possibility of love swelled in my chest as I held her gaze.

"Ready?" I said.

Chapter 12

"Could you help with my dating profile?" my mother asked. "It's on the computer and you know those damn things, I can never figure out what to do." She rolled her eyes and screwed up her face at me. A couple of years had passed since we had reconciled after my father's death and I was at her home in Florida. We sat side by side in front of an old desk she had meticulously refurbished, painted with swirls of gold filigree and delicate flowers.

I fired up her old desktop, sat back to wait as it whirred and beeped.

"Match.com, right?" I asked, pulling up the site, finding her profile.

"Sixty-two?" I queried. "It says here you're sixty-two."

"Well, yes," she said, a defiant set to her jaw.

"But that's ten years younger," I said.

"It isn't a crime," she said, her hazel eyes flashing. "You think I want to date old alte cockers my age, or even older? What for?" Her voice rose to a high octave. "So I can take them to their doctor's appointments and dole out their pills three times a day? Who needs that?"

"I see your point," I ventured on. "But don't you think they'll catch on that you're lying?"

"What?" she glared at me. "You think I look my age? No one else says I do."

I knew my mother was sensitive about her looks, which had always been held up as her crowning glory.

"Wish I could trade myself in for a new model," she'd said the day before, as if she was an Edsel. She'd stood in front of a full-length mirror at T-J Maxx, torso twisted to see how her butt looked in a pair of pants she contemplated purchasing. "I used to have more padding back there," she sighed. "Flat as a pancake now."

"My god," she said, turning to face the mirror. "Who is that wrinkled old bag?"

My mother had been a model for Symplicity Patterns back in her twenties. Classically beautiful, her cheekbones were prominent, her nose small and straight, her tall body lean and compact.

"My boss at Symplicity would only use my body." She'd told the story many times over the years. "Had to pay you more if they used your face. I got cut off at the neck. Can you imagine?" Her voice would rise in indignation. "Cheapskates!"

I knew aging and its consequent sagging and wrinkling were a gross affrontery to her sense of self.

"I only go to dimly lit parties," she'd often quip, with a choked laugh and sad eyes.

I turned back to the computer, treading carefully around the topic of age.

"Okay, fine," I said. "Sixty-two. But you'll be starting out a relationship with a lie."

"What re-la-tion-ship?" she said, spacing out each syllable mockingly. "I just want someone to pal around with, go to the movies."

"Sixty-two it is," I said. "Next question. What are your hobbies?"

"Flirting and dancing," she said quickly. Obviously, she had been thinking about the questions.

Flirting and dancing, I typed, not meeting her eyes.

The next day I returned to my San Diego home, three thousand miles away from my mother.

"How's the dating going?" I asked during one of our weekly phone conversations.

"Unbelievable, these men," she said. "I met one at a coffee shop and he showed up wearing short shorts, gym shorts, like you'd wear to, well, to the gym, of course." I imagined her twisting her lips to one side and rolling her eyes. "Can you believe it? And his t-shirt, looked like he'd just rolled out of bed, food stains, disgusting. And flip flops. He bought my coffee at least, but really, that was the end of that." She heaved a big sigh.

By our next conversation, things were looking up.

"Handsome," she said.

"Oh, wow," I said encouragingly. "What does he do?"

"He has a laundromat in Delray. Bought it last year when he moved here from Brazil."

"He's Brazilian?" I asked.

"No, American." She was quiet for a few seconds. "He's quite a bit younger than me."

"How old?" I asked.

"Fifty-two," she said. "Of course, he thinks I'm only sixty-two."

"Guess he likes older women," I said.

"Probably not as old as I really am," she said. "But I'm not going to tell him my real age."

A week later my mother had more details about her new beau.

"He's got two kids back in Brazil," she said.

"He's divorced?" I asked.

"Not exactly." After a long pause she added, "She's a lot younger. He sends them money. He's always pinching pennies."

"He's married with two kids in Brazil?" I asked.

"You could say so."

"I could say so? Yes or no?"

"Yes, but, you know men."

"And you?" I asked. "How's that all sit with you?"

I heard her sigh.

"I like having him around," she said.

I held my tongue and didn't ask any more questions.

*

Now, in light of the revelations of lies and deception that permeated every aspect of our relationship, I realized my mother had an intimate familiarity and comfort with fabrication and prevarication. Lying to prospective beaus no doubt came easy. And I, having sensed, at some level, since childhood, the disconnection caused by unspoken truths, had developed a heightened hunger for truth and integrity.

Chapter 13

August passed. Fall began. Five months since my cousin had spilled the beans and told me Louie wasn't my father. Four months since "Italian" had shown up in my DNA profile and, although I'd been matched to dozens of third to fifth cousins, still nothing concrete came from my Ancestry.com or 23andMe queries. My spirits were low as I neared my sixty-seventh birthday.

I had uploaded my raw DNA data to GEDMATCH.com, a free, large database and also signed up with FamilytreeDNA.com. The more data bases my DNA was compared with, the greater chance I'd be paired with someone who'd also bought into that same data base. In other words, if my father or half-sibling signed up with a company that I hadn't signed up with, our data would be orbiting in cyberspace, near each other, but never overlapping, like some of the planets in a Kandinsky print, *The Universe: Creation, Constellations and the Cosmos*, that hung on my bedroom wall. The largest globe in the print, translucent yellow shadowed in black, was overlapped by three smaller orbs. My eyes were drawn to this shared space of the planets, a Venn diagram. The singular globes, in their discrete colors of orange, purple, red and blue, orbited on the periphery of the print. They drifted, searching, like me. I yearned for my own Venn diagram, an overlap with my paternal family.

"Aren't there professionals who do this sort of thing?" my husband asked one morning at breakfast after I'd described my lack of progress. "Like on those TV shows?" We'd watched "Who Do You Think You Are?" and "Long Lost Family" on TV, seen celebrities react to the revelation of family secrets and new blood relatives, witnessed tearful reunions.

"Genealogists, sure."

"And couldn't you hire one?"

What a concept! Pay someone to help me? My usual way was to go it alone, figure things out for myself, make a to-do list, tackle the items one by one, check off the boxes, and move on.

But my usual way wasn't working and here was a possible solution. Find a genealogist! Of course, that was the ticket!

Happy to have a concrete task, back to my laptop I went, googling genealogists. Ancestry.com offered genealogy researchers and I spoke with Devon, who told me right away that I only had fifteen minutes of his time on this first, free-of-charge call. After I gave him a brief re-cap of what I'd found out so far, he explained that in addition to the DNA matches, he'd investigate the birth, death, marriage and census records of my identified cousins, honing in on clues. He anticipated the search for my bio dad would take two to six months, at a cost of $2,700 to find him and $3,900 if I also wanted to identify my paternal grandparents. When I expressed shock at the price, he assured me I'd get money back if they found my paternal roots quicker than anticipated. I decided to keep looking.

My next call was to Lineages, the company that produces Finding Your Roots on PBS.

During a long, relaxed conversation with Nick Sheedy, he emphasized the importance of my sister Vicki, who I now knew was genetically my maternal half-sister, and her DNA's role in my search.

"If she'll agree to have her DNA tested, I can rule out any people you and she share DNA with," he explained.

"Why would that help?" I asked.

"Because people you and your sister have in common could only be from your maternal side," he said. "And we're interested only in your paternal side, which would not share DNA with your sister's relatives, so I could ignore those people when searching for yours. It'd save me a lot of time."

He went on to say my birth certificate was probably sealed, not destroyed, and that my birth hospital may still have my records. Lineages would ask for them. And because they are a reputable company, doors often open to them that would be closed to most people. Likewise, he might have more luck in reaching out to Linda D., whom Ancestry.com identified as my "probable first cousin", than I had.

"I've found that folks are often reluctant to believe the stories of random, unknown people they hear from online," he said. "When I call, and identify myself as a Lineages representative, they feel safe to open up."

I felt heard and understood by this warm, caring person, and when he said the price for his services was $750 for a ten-hour block of research, I signed up immediately, which entailed filling out a detailed questionnaire and attaching a copy of my amended birth certificate.

I was elated that I had a competent ally on my side to solve the mystery of my biological father.

Nick emailed a few days later and wrote:

> "I looked at the 1951 Manhattan Birth Index (which would reflect how names appear on the birth certificate as it was originally filed), and find you as Regina Podnieck, born on the same date, and the certificate number matches – see attached document. So your surname on your original birth certificate was your mother's maiden name, which means your biological father's name was very likely not given on your original birth certificate. We cannot order your original certificate anyway, since it is sealed (or possibly destroyed). But it would not help identify your biological father."

I printed Nick's attachment and held the first concrete proof I'd ever actually had in my hands, a paper with weight, not a computer image, confirming that Louie was not my biological father. Barely legible, and smudged around the border with grey ink, the paper felt almost holy in my hand. My name, Podniek, Regina, the first name listed under "Births reported in the city of New York – 1951". My mother's maiden name was my original surname!

Nick also wrote that he would not do much more investigating until my sister's DNA results came in, so as to make the best use of my research time (and money). And given that the holidays were fast approaching, and genealogy research had become a popular holiday gift, my project may have to be delayed until he plowed through the backlog of projects he was already working on. My excitement deflated as I realized I was in for what, to me, seemed an interminable wait.

Chapter 14

"I never had much of a childhood," Louie once said to me. "Kids didn't get much attention back then. We just grew up. I never even had a birthday party."

Born to Polish immigrants in the lower east side of New York in 1909, his family of five children grew up poor. "Not a pot to piss in," he would say. One of his sisters died in infancy. He quit high school, rode freight cars across America and got odd jobs on freighters to travel the seas. He never spoke much of those days and usually answered my inquires in a distracted, off-handed manner, absorbed in his newspapers, the price of gasoline and Adele Davis regimes, recipes for healthy living. Slight of build, he always worried about his cholesterol level.

Over the years I learned parts of my father's story. In the 1930s he took courses in Morse code and upgraded his skills to become a radio operator. He changed his name from Markowitz to March because the Maritime Union wasn't hiring Jews, then joined the Merchant Marines to sail the world. With his penchant for linguistics, he became fluent in five languages.

After WWII he lived in Warsaw and then Vienna, a civilian officer, working for Radio Free Europe. He was always tight-lipped with details, and for years I thought he had been a secret agent, adding to his unknowable, mysterious aura. During my high school graduation trip to Europe in 1969, my mother, father, sister and I visited the apartment building in Vienna where he had lived, a rectangular, blocky, stone edifice in a row of others. We had coffee and pastry with an old woman who had remained in the same rooms since the war. The air was stale and every square inch of the ornate furniture was covered with doilies, framed photographs and glass animal figurines. I was itching to leave. My father and his old friend reminisced on and on about the food and chocolates he once brought her from the officer's mess when rations were scarce. We finally said our goodbyes. As we left the building, my father looked up towards a balcony.

"That's where it happened," he said to my mother. "She landed right here, where I'm standing now."

"Who landed there?" I asked. My mother glared at him, biting her lip and shaking her head. He took his cue and didn't answer. Hands clasped behind his back, he walked a few paces in front of us towards the train station. Years later I extracted a morsel of the story from my mother. His lover had leapt from the balcony after he ended their affair. At the time of my mother's telling, I cast my father as the charismatic, compelling leading man in a romantic war movie. What power he had! His lover killed herself rather than live without him. I added Casanova to the list of his enigmas.

Returning to New York City, my father continued to "ship out", as he called it, working first for the Merchant Marines and then for the Radio Corporation of America (RCA) as a ship-to-shore radio operator. I was told he met my mother in 1950 at the Loreli Bar on 86th Street in Manhattan, a popular spot with German speaking New Yorkers.

"Our first date was at the automat," my mother, laughing, answered my question about their history as a couple. I must have been in my thirties and curious about their history. Horn and Hardart, a cafeteria that offered prepared foods behind small glass windows and coin-operated slots, was a popular fixture in New York City at the time.

"If I was lucky, he'd buy me a cup of coffee," she said. "If not, he'd fill a coffee cup with hot water, add ketchup, and call it tomato soup."

"We got married at City Hall," my mother added.

"Who else was there?" I asked.

"No one else, just us."

Once, when I was five years old, my father took us on a tour of the U.S.S. Constitution, a luxury passenger liner docked in New York awaiting a new crew. I have a photograph of the two of us on the deck of the ship. I'm dressed in a starched pinafore dress, atop his shoulders. His arms are raised to grasp me around my ankles, his white shirt rolled up on his forearms. He has a rueful, self-conscious smile on his handsome face, wide cheekbones, a high forehead capped with wavy, dark hair. It's one of only a few photos I have of physical contact between the two of us.

I remember being in awe of my father that day and feeling I was important, too, just by being with him. With the ease of a sleepwalker, he led the way around the ship, first on the royal red plush carpets of the upper decks, through the chandeliered grand foyers, our reflections mirrored on shiny brass guardrails and just-washed windows. Leaving the luxury of the upper decks for the working area of the ship, we traipsed down spiral stairways with cold metal handrails, our footsteps echoing down passageways so narrow we had to walk single file, the stale air smelling of cooked lima beans. The deeper into the belly of the ship we went, the louder the exposed pipes above our heads clanged and hissed like strangled cats and dinner gongs.

"We're here," my father said as he turned to me and took my hand. I had to step high to clear the bottom of the rusted, heavy, oval door he pushed open to the radio room. Inside were beeping instrument panels, wavy lines traversing what looked like television screens.

"Hi, Sparks." A man with his back to us, wearing headphone like winter earmuffs, turned to wave. His mouth was full and the room smelled of liverwurst. I found out this was where my father lived his life when he wasn't with us.

My mother and I would await his postcards and letters, postmarked Lisbon, Athens, Tokyo, Bangkok, Karachi and follow his journey on the map on our kitchen wall. Once we got a photograph of him standing alone in a foreign street, his hands deep in his suit pockets, a top hat perched on his head. Lampposts with pointed glass tops like the ones in my Cinderella storybook lined the sidewalk behind him.

I never knew what was behind his decision to take a land job, but when I was seven years old we moved from the Bronx to the east coast of southern Florida and my father drove to the same drab building every day to work as the shore component to the ship-to-shore Morse code communication used by seafaring vessels. After the adventure of world travel, his world narrowed and to me he seemed diminished and depressed most of the time. He had little in common with the men in our neighborhood who talked sports and cars at potluck dinners in shabby Veteran of Foreign Wars clubs. My father turned inward to his books and memories. Once a week my family would visit the public library and he'd exit with a pile of history books in his arms, his chin resting atop the pile to steady the load.

"He wrote the first anti-smoking book, long before they were popular," my mother told me a few years after his death in 1995. "Researched all the medical books. Knew all the facts before anyone else put them all together. But when he brought it to a publisher they said 'who are you, anyway? You're not even a doctor'. That book, and a novel he wrote and kept under the bed, they both went into the garbage."

*

"Go stand in front of the bookcase for a photo," my mother said when my date arrived to take me to the high school senior prom.

The bookcase, nestled in a corner of a lanai added onto our modest Florida tract home, was custom built by my father and crafted to accommodate the oversized height of the Encyclopedia Britannica. Often a backdrop for photos, the encyclopedia had a big presence in our lives. My usually skeptical father purchased the reference books from a door-to-door salesman, and one day large cardboard boxes arrived at our door. There were twenty-six volumes wrapped in white tissue paper, one for each letter of the alphabet and an index volume, each one a large, hefty tome requiring two hands to lift. We unwrapped the books with reverence, and I remember the feel of my fingers tracing the textured burgundy covers, the heavy cardboard embossed like expensive paper, important feeling. The spine of each volume was etched with the one gold letter of the alphabet. Each volume had a silky tassel as a page marker, the paper pages tissue thin, almost translucent. My father handled each book with awe, placed it reverently on its handcrafted shelf.

My dad would sit for hours on the swivel light blue upholstered chair in the lanai, reading the encyclopedia. Sixteen years older than my mother, already in his mid-fifties when I entered my teenage years, his frame gaunt and dark hair thin over his temples, he'd hover a boney finger over the page, ready to be wetted by his tongue and used to flick to the next page. He started with volume "A" and proceeded, by the time I was 18 and no longer living at home, through "L".

"The Etruscans were a powerful civilization in Europe long before the Romans," my father said one evening at the dinner table. He would often produce an obscure fact out of the blue. No response or answer was expected. The message was clear. Knowing was important; knowing how things worked, knowing history, being smart was everything. Knowing could keep us safe, set us apart from the non-knowers, the riff-raff, the "masses of asses" my dad was so quick to denigrate. I was confused by the vehemence of his condemnation of the majority of the world population. I liked my friends' parents. What did that say about me? Would I grow up to be a regular, unimportant person?

I so much wanted to gain my father's approval, to be thought smart and special by him. As a high school student, I made a show of reading the encyclopedia, lounging on the sofa with a heavy tome propped on my stomach. Maybe if I ate those translucent pages, crammed my mouth and body with words, those all-impressive words, swallowed them whole, then maybe, when I opened my mouth anew, beautiful, deep, original brilliant sentences would usher from my lips and stun him, impress him, make him notice me, make him call me his precious daughter.

*

"Don't you think they look alike?" I placed a photo of my father and one of my son, Eli, on the table in front of my mother. It was several years after we'd reconciled and she was visiting me in San Diego. My father's photo, identified in his handwriting as Zacopani, Poland, 1937, on the back, showed him full-cheeked, with a hint of a smile, close cropped hair and a slightly bent nose. He would have been twenty-seven years old. Eli, in his photo, was clad in a tux and bow tie for his high-school senior yearbook photo and grinned a self-conscious grin.

"Don't you think the cut of their jaw is similar? Their cheekbones?" I looked at my mother. Her face was expressionless. "Don't you?" I urged.

She looked away, spread a cloth dinner napkin out flat on the table. Refolded it.

"Mom?" I put the two photos side by side on top of the napkin, pushed them toward her.

"Maybe," she said. "Eli's face is still unformed. He's young." She pushed her chair back and stood up.

Puzzled, I sat there, slack jawed. My mother often berated me for not reminiscing about my father, who by then had been dead ten years. "You never bring Louie up," she'd said. "You'd think he never existed the way you ignore his memory." She was right. I seldom had anything good to say about the father who disowned me, so I didn't talk about him often. Here I had an upbeat connection to celebrate. Why wasn't she enthusiastic about these photos, why wasn't she gushing over the likeness of her husband and grandson?

In light of the revelations about my birth father, I of course now knew the reason. Louie and her grandson Eli were not genetically related. I was fabricating a facial similarity between them. Was she tired of the lies, contemplating spilling the beans? Those photos would have been a perfect opportunity to tell me the truth. What compelled her to continue lying?

Chapter 15

Painted in bright primary colors, the Expressive Arts on 32nd Street Studio lit up a corner of the trendy South Park neighborhood in San Diego. The door, festooned with bells and papered with the studio's schedule of classes, tinkled as I pushed it open. It was early Fall of 2018, six months since I'd found out that Louie wasn't my biological father.

"Welcome," a woman stuck out her hand to me as soon as I entered. "I'm Tish." Her short hair, blond and frosted with a magenta streak on both sides, was tucked behind her ears. She had a wide-open smile which lit up her blue eyes, and warmth that radiated from her whole being.

"So this is your studio?" I asked.

"Yep, my baby." Her eyes lingered on mine and I imagined she read the hesitation behind my gaze, my reluctance to stay. "C'mon in. Take a look around before you sit down."

I circled the periphery of the space, feigned interest in the art as my mind swirled, debating whether or not to join the group, a weekly drop-in, entitled Women's Expression Session, that I'd read about on-line. "Make art that changes your life," the website had exclaimed. "No previous art background needed. A safe place to explore your creativity."

A large table and chairs took up most of the main room of the studio. The walls were covered with art – small ceramic sculptures, large canvases splashed with abstract color, a spider-web like sculpture made from twisted plastic, so big that it hung from the ceiling in one corner and touched the floor. In a smaller room off to the side a tall cabinet, its wood doors flung open, burst with large plastic bottles of tempera paint on shelves, smaller paint containers in open drawers, and a potpourri of art-making paraphernalia stacked haphazardly in the corners. The walls of this room were themselves splashed with paint, layers of it, and the smell of the acrylics and tempera brought to mind my son's kindergarten classroom of days past. The whole studio seemed a controlled chaos, vibrant and bristling with energy.

I had been told by a therapist years before that I was very "in my head", very analytical, and would benefit from connecting more to my heart. I didn't know what that meant, exactly. Thinking and figuring things out were always my strengths. I was always searching, searching for answers to questions of how I fit into the world. I gravitated towards theories - psychology, sociology, politics; systems that gave me structure, parameters to establish boundaries on how to think and act. In addition, they gave me right and wrong answers, black and white solutions. A way to "know" how to order my life.

But thinking hadn't done me much good lately. I still wrestled with the question of how big of a deal was it to find out the father who raised me, who I'd met when I was three, was not my biological father; I'd found out the truth at sixty-six years old; my mother never told me; my "father" had disowned me and accused me of being crazy. Was I supposed to move on with life? Or should I linger here? Feel this discomfort? "Work"on it? Round and round my thoughts spun, going nowhere.

I still felt lethargic, and knew I was teetering into depression. It seemed my feelings resided deeper inside myself than my brain could access - in my bone marrow, in the miniscule strands of DNA squirreled away in my cells, in the fascia, the translucent, thin layer of tissue stretching throughout my whole body, wrapping each muscle and nerve, connecting me from head to toe.

Some survival instinct in me urged "try something new, something different". My default was all left brain, analytical. Maybe my right brain held the key to accessing whatever I needed to move through this chapter in my life. Maybe creativity could help me connect to my heart.

I took a seat at the table in Tish's studio, joining several women who seemed to know each other and were chatting amiably. Tish started the session with a poem followed by a "dong" on a Tibetan bowl, and invited the eight of us seated around the table to say, briefly, how we were doing, how our week had been. She passed a "talking stick", and asked us to refrain from commenting on each other's remarks during the circle. Coming from my political activism background, my first reaction to all this was skepticism and a touch of embarrassment at how contrived the scene seemed. We were strangers after all, at least I was. How open could we be with each other?

But my pessimism quickly evaporated as I listened to the stories shared. Janna, a woman a few years older than I, with white hair cut in a bob, teased slightly on top, and startling blue eyes, told of the stroke her husband suffered ten years before and of her struggle, as his main caregiver, to assert her own needs into their daily routines. Susan, the youngest in our group, model-thin, with classic facial features to match and shoulder-length brown hair, spoke of her teenage son, deeply depressed and failing at school. I was struck by the openness and vulnerability of the speakers, the safety that existed in the room for honesty and acceptance. And, most amazing to me, was that the women, who at my first impression seemed very well put-together, happy and well-functioning, were struggling with such deep emotional issues.

As the talking stick came closer to me, I got more and more nervous. Did I belong here? How would my story be received? Did I dare open up?

I stumbled through my turn, describing my discovery about my father who was not my birth father, and the last few months of trying to cope with the news. The faces looking back at me wore expressions of empathy and concern. When the sharing circle ended and we began moving around the studio to collect materials for our art-making, several women commented privately to me how shocking my news must have been. Maybe my story really was a big deal after all. My core trembled as I released one shaky breath after another.

"Magazines for collages, yarn and pastels are in here." Tish, giving me a quick tour of the studio, pointed out a tiny room, shelves crammed with materials.

"I'm not sure where to start," I said.

"Try going through some magazines, look for images that speak to you, that reflect how you're feeling. Don't over-think it. Just tear them out, several of them, and then glue them onto your page in whichever way seems satisfying to you," she paused, looking in my eyes again with that direct way she had, and smiled. "It's the process that counts, not the product. No judgement here."

Week after week, I kept being drawn back to the women's group at the studio. I watched and learned what "expressive art" meant. One morning I arrived roiled up and tearful after a poor night's sleep. The down beat of the music, an Afro-Cuban rhythm, lent an evocative pulse to the air.

I stood, feet planted wider than hip-width, a brush heavy with red tempera paint, its tip swollen, about to drip, in one hand. Earlier, I had painted both pages of my open journal a deep black, dried the pages with a hair-dryer, and propped the book on a chair against the paint-splashed wall in the studio. I aimed at that empty, vacant black background, a dark hole, a starless night. My arm swooped up, up above my head, and on the down swing I lunged forward with one foot, snapped the paint off the brush at the void. Splat – a gash of red, angry red, popped off the black.

Another brush, primary yellow. I was sweating, not hearing the music any more, only peripherally aware of others in the room. That stance again. Rooted. Arm up, lunge, thwap – a comets tail whipped the page with bold yellow. A roar in my head, as if I held a conch shell to my ear. I breathed hard, my mouth awash with saliva. Again, arm up, a flick of my wrist splashed another parabola of yellow. Molten lava seemed to flow from my toes to my fingers clutching the paintbrush.

Again: orange. Again: green. Again: blue. Slash, slash, slash.

I dried the pages with the hair dryer, slowed my breathing, wiped my eyes and returned to my seat. I ripped letters out of a magazine, glued them down over the riot of color: I HAD THE RIGHT TO KNOW, across the whole page. The refrain that had played, over and over and over again in my mind was now on the page, a foreground for the vivid splash, slash, arcs of color on the black abyss. A surge of satisfaction pulsed up my spine. I breathed deep and sat back in my chair, able to rejoin the group of women working around me.

Chapter 16

Christmas and the New Year's Day came and went without any word from Lineages. In late January, after leaving messages on his phone, I got a phone call from Nick.

"I'm ready to reach out to Linda D. now and also check into your other close DNA matches," he said. "By mid-February all the DNA kits purchased as Christmas presents should be processed, expanding the possibility more relatives of yours are identified."

Later that same day, Nick emailed.

> "I did a little digging and determined that your "1st cousin" match at Ancestry, Linda D., was likely born in the 1940s. She appears to be the daughter of John Ferrino and Dominica Giordano who married in 1938 in New Rochelle, New York."

He went on to list Linda's paternal grandparents (Ferrinos) and maternal grandparents (Giodanos), all born in Italy.

"If you and Linda are indeed first-cousins (as your DNA match suggests), then your father is either one of John Ferrino's four brothers, or he was Joseph Giordano."

And a few hours later, another email from Nick:

"I followed up on the leads and determined that you do not match any other people with the surname Ferrino in their family trees. But you match MANY distant cousins with the surname Giordano in their family trees. This strongly suggests you are related to the Giordano (and not the Ferrino) family.

This is pointing to your biological father being Joseph Giordano (born 1921 in New York), the only known son of Bruno Giordano (born 1889 in Italy) and his wife Angelina (born 1897 in Italy).

There were at least a couple men named Joseph Giordano who were born around 1921 and lived in New Rochelle, New York. I am sending out some search requests and inquiries and we will see where they get us."

Giordano. My paternal family at last! Was my father Joseph still alive? Did I have any sisters or brothers? A google search found many Joseph Giordanos, Giordano pizza chains, a frozen pizza company, a bike store. I decided to let Nick narrow down which Giordanos I belonged to.

But two days later, Nick sent this correction:

"I heard back from some cousins of Linda D., and we have made progress.

You are not closely related to the Giordano side of Linda's family. You are closely related to her Ferrino side of the family.

Linda's paternal grandparents were James/Vincent Ferrino (born @ 1885 in Italy) and his wife Angelina (born @ 1890 in Italy). They would also be your grandparents.

This couple had five sons, Joseph, John, Thomas, Ernest and Francis and they also had four daughters, Fannie, Anna, Raphaella and Margaret.

I heard back from another cousin, Carol T. She is the daughter of your aunt Fannie (born @ 1913). Carol believes that your father was her uncle Ernest "Ernie" Ferrino who was born about 1917 and died in 1969. Ernest was in the Navy during World War II and was a merchant marine after the war. He then lived in New Rochelle and Larchmont, New York, and worked in New York City as a painter who put up billboards. Ernest never married and had no known children. Carol said he was a great guy, and she knew him well. She thinks she has a photo of him in his sailor uniform. Carol is willing to visit and share family information. It sounds like other Ferrino cousins are not interested to be involved.

I have gathered a few documents on the Ferrino family and Ernest in particular. We need to wait on Carol to share what she might have. Feel free to give me a call if you'd like to discuss these developments."

My thoughts see-sawed, Giordano vs Ferrino, as I tried to make sense of this new information.

"How can you be so sure I'm from Ferrino side?" were the first words out of my mouth when Nick answered my call.

"I reached out to the Giordanos, and their DNA profiles were not a strong match to yours. So you're not on that side of the family."

"But how can you be so sure of the Ferrino connection?" I asked, not wanting to be led down another false path. This time I wanted fool-proof evidence.

"Your DNA connection to them is much stronger. And I spoke to Carol, Linda D.'s first cousin."

"Why didn't you speak directly to Linda?" I asked.

"When I contacted her, she didn't want to be involved. She didn't really want her DNA tested in the first place, but agreed to do it when her nephew asked her to. She never even saw your query to her in the ancestry.com message box. But after I spoke with her, Linda called her cousin Carol, who she knew was compiling a family tree, and told her about your search. Carol got in touch with me right away. She confirmed that cottonmike5, listed as your second to fifth cousin on ancestry, is her nephew, so his mother is a first cousin of Linda D."

I remembered that name, cottonmike5. He and I had corresponded briefly after he answered my query in the ancestry.com message box. But neither of us knew enough about genealogy to figure out our connection. So I had had the key to my paternal family since July! I just hadn't known it.

"When I told Carol that your father was, according to your mother's niece, 'a sailor from upstate New York'", Nick said, "Carol said one of her uncles, Ernest Ferrino, was a sailor, the only sailor in his family of five brothers. He lived in New Rochelle and Larchmont, north of New York City. And he was in the Merchant Marines until 1954."

"How can we be sure my father wasn't one of the other four brothers?" I said.

"We can't," he said. "Not unless the children of those brothers would agree to be tested. But they don't seem to want to be involved, so this isn't a good time to push it. Besides, if your mother's niece is correct, and your father was a sailor, Ernest was the only sailor in his family. That, plus the DNA matches, certainly points in his direction."

I let Nick's information course through me, wave after wave of relief at finally knowing the truth and then waves of grief at finally knowing that same truth. My father was dead. I would never look into his eyes. I had five paternal uncles and four aunts. Were any of them still alive? Did any of them know the story of Ernest and my mother? Of me? My grandparents, James and Angelina, came to the US from Italy. I existed because they existed. All this was true, whether I had ever known about them or not. The murky water of secrets and deceptions was beginning to clear. What more would I uncover about my paternal family history?

Chapter 17

"My father died when I was three years old," my mother said. She and I were walking along the La Jolla coastline, a frequent ritual when she came to visit me after we'd reconciled.

"I found him on the sofa. I thought he was asleep, climbed up onto his chest, tried to wake him up. Shook him and shook him. He had had a massive heart attack. He was only in his early forties."

I always walked on my mother's left, her left elbow snug against my waist, our fingers interlaced, forearms at a right angle to our bodies. Gauging my mother's energy on any particular day, I'd match my stride to hers. Hearing the sadness in her voice that day, I stopped and turned to face her.

"Must have been so hard to see him that way," I said, looking into her eyes.

"My mother was completely dependent on him," she went on as if I hadn't spoken, nudged me with her elbow, urging me to keep walking. "Remember, he had brought her to Latvia from Poland, and she didn't even speak Latvian. When he died, she had to take in wash from the neighbors to make enough money to feed us - Tessie, Peter and me. I was the youngest and was her translator and went around the neighborhood, knocking on doors, collecting money. We just barely scrapped by."

Again, I made an empathetic comment, and this time she just kept on walking, eyes straight ahead, quiet for a few moments.

"What good does it do to remember?" she finally said. "The past is the past."

*

In the years following our reconciliation, I made a conscious effort to learn more about my mother's and grandmother's histories, their years during WWII in Latvia, their flight from Latvia to displaced persons camps in Germany, and their immigration to the United States. My mother told those stories when I was a child, but then they'd had the effect of shutting down my curiosity rather than piquing it.

"You'll eat whatever I give you," she'd command at the dinner table when I was a kid, plopping liver and onions on my plate. "In the camps all we had to eat were cold potatoes, with their black eyes staring us in the face. I'd gag just at the site of the them. You don't know how lucky you are."

Don't blame me for those damn potatoes, my anger would smolder, always unspoken. I wasn't even born yet, I'd fume inside.

I was growing up in the sheltered soil of Florida in the 1960s. I wanted Mr. Pants, madras skirts and a record player in my bedroom to listen to the Beatles. I wanted car rides with my friends to Sean Connery movies and Dairy Queen sundaes. I didn't want to hear her stories. They meant I was guilty of wanting too much, guilty of causing that pained look on her face, guilty of having it too good.

"My mother," my mother recounted, "she depended on me. I took care of her since I was a little girl. She was Polish and in Latvia, the Latvians looked down on her. She didn't know the language so well. I was the one to go to the landlord to ask him not to raise the rent. And then, when we were in the camps in Germany, she had no skills, no way to earn money. All they would give her to do was peel potatoes. I tried to protect her from that. I could speak four languages. The German commanders, they noticed things like that. They gave me a job as a translator for their torpedo factory. I supported my mother, to save her the humiliation of peeling potatoes in the damp, dirty kitchens. She depended on me."

And me? What kind of daughter was I? I wanted my freedom – to smoke dope, hang out with my long-haired boyfriends on the beach. I had a job at the Eagle Army-Navy store after school, enough money to pay insurance on the 1963 Dodge Dart my parents bought me, enough money for gas and clothes.

I saved enough to go to San Francisco for the summer with a friend. I was eighteen and my mother was against the trip, but I insisted. Guilt and anger flared in me when I saw the hurt look on my mother's face. It meant her pain was my fault. Still, I resented any responsibility to make her happy.

I hadn't yet discovered how WWII was sitting between us like a mushroom cloud, present always with its devastating consequences, yet transparent after strong shifting winds blew away the radioactive traces.

As decades passed, my mother's aging, and mine alongside her, finally opened a thirst in me to know her history. I understood better as the years went by the enormity of the journey she'd made from a penniless refugee to a middle-class US citizen. During our cross-country visits, I'd always have a tape recorder handy, in case she was in the mood to talk and answer my questions. Sometimes her stories came in bursts of loquaciousness and she'd tell them in great detail, as if remembering what happened only last week. She seemed ageless then, as if she were using the facial muscles of her seventeen-year-old self to move her eyes and mouth to see and speak in present day. I'd transcribe the stories once I had a few. I wanted a hard copy of her experiences so I could make concrete all the subtle ways they had influenced me. I hoped the better I understood her past, the reasons behind her demanding, controlling behavior, the less I would be triggered by the barbs she aimed at me.

Chapter 18

"Do you FaceTime?" Carol, my newly discovered Italian first cousin in New Jersey said as soon as she answered my call. It was the day after Nick, my genealogist, told me Ernest Ferrino was my biological father.

When I called her, I was in my car, in the parking lot of a funeral home and cemetery miles from my house, having just attended a memorial for the son of a friend. I had been so anxious to talk with Carol that, when Nick told me the time she proposed for our call, I'd said yes, knowing I wouldn't be home. I'd parked beneath a line of tall eucalyptus trees, their branches, akimbo at odd angles, offering shade from the afternoon's hot sun.

"FaceTime, good idea," I answered Carol quickly.

A friendly face, eyes brightened by a smile, appeared on my cell-phone. I'd been holding my breath and, seeing her disposition, I exhaled, relieved.

"You look like one of us," Carol said after we both hesitated a beat.

"Our hair," I touched my head.

"Salt and pepper, right?" she said. Carol's hair, cut in a bob, was a bit wavier than mine. Chubby cheeked, she had a wide-open face and a direct gaze.

"Did you know about me?" I asked. It was the question most on my mind once I'd found out about this new family. Had they known I'd existed? Had they known about my mother?

"I had no idea," her voice trailed off. "Ernie never married, didn't have any children."

"Surprise! He had me," I paused, embarrassed by my nervous guffaw.

Carol stopped smiling. I wasn't sure how to proceed.

"We didn't know," she continued. "My mother, Fannie, was closet to Ernie of all the siblings, so if anyone would've known, she would have. I'll never know for sure if she did or not. She died three years ago. All of the nine brothers and sisters, my aunts and uncles, are gone now, may they rest in peace."

My heart sank. I had so wished someone was alive who might know the story of my mother and father.

"What was Ernie like?" I asked.

"He was a funny guy, nice, caring, always kind, the sort of person who helped anybody," Carol said. "I knew him best of all my uncles. He was over at my house all the time. He had a dog he loved a lot, a cocker spaniel, Mr. Chips was his name."

I brushed tears off my cheeks. "I wish I could've met him," I managed to say.

"He died too young," she said. "Only 53. A massive heart-attack. At work. He worked putting up the big billboards."

Carol went on to tell me about all my aunts and uncles, what they did for a living, how many kids they had.

"With you," she said, "there are nineteen of us first cousins."

I vacillated between feeling numb and tearful, unable to fully take in the magnitude of the event unfolding in my car, such a strange place to be having this conversation. I was talking with, and staring at, my father's niece. She was kind, seemed to fully accept me as a new member of her family. The anxiety I'd been carrying all day began to lift off my body, my sweaty hand unclenched and I fumbled with the phone.

"Could I come visit you?" I held my breath awaiting her answer. Carol was seventy-nine years old and I feared a medical crisis would prevent me from ever meeting her in person. I was ready to jump on an airplane the next day. I didn't want to wait another minute to be in the same room with her, hear more family stories, get a look at what my life might have been like had I remained in the Ferrino family.

"Maybe the end of April would work," she said quickly, as if she had thought of the answer in advance in case I asked. "My siblings and cousins who live in Florida usually come to New York in April or May. Some of them might want to meet you."

April or May? It was only the beginning of February! But I remembered what Nick told me. "Don't push it. The news may be a lot for the family to take in."

"Sounds good," I lied.

"In the meantime, I'll email you a photo of Ernie. I also have his death certificate and our grandmother's birth certificate."

We made plans to stay in touch and said goodbye.

So that was that. All the anticipation, the months of waiting, drained out of me. The shadows of the trees had shifted and my car was now baked by the sun, uncomfortably warm inside. I collapsed back in the seat, stunned, too heavy-limbed to consider driving away. A second later, I burst into tears of relief. Carol had welcomed me into her family. Then grief wrestled to the surface. I'd never meet my father, the kind, caring man Carol described. I'd never hear his voice. We'd never have the chance to compare the bend of our noses, the curve of our ears. We'd never have the chance to marvel at a similar foot-fall in our stride or maybe even our penchant for an obscure spice or any of the other marvels I'd read about that can happen when long-separated parents and offspring meet. I'd never have a moment of time with him.

No one was alive to tell me the story of my mother and father. How they met. Why they parted. Whether I was conceived in love or a random sexual encounter. I'd been given a shadowed, obscured, incomplete peek at my origins. Any details would remain conjecture. Secrets would remain untold. A photo of my father was all I'd get. A death-certificate. I'd have to make do, live with the unknown.

A bitter-sweet, familiar heaviness settled deeper in my gut, a weight of confusion and despair. I'd had my hopes up, and although the meeting with Carol had gone well, I still felt let down. I'd learned so much, yet knew so little.

*

I printed a copy of the black and white photo of Ernie Carol emailed to me. At first glance, I couldn't see a resemblance between him and me at all. He looked to be in his forties, an overweight looking guy, the photo only from the chest on up. He had fleshy, chubby cheeks, a five-o'clock shadow that gave him sort of a thuggish look. Prominent in the photo were his heavy-framed, black glasses, blocking his eyebrows and the tops of his eyes. I imagined the glasses left an indentation on his nose and he'd often have to take them off to massage the bridge between his eyes. He had a Mona Lisa smile, thin lips slightly upturned at the corners. He seemed to be in on something funny, to be looking at the photographer with a knowing look, a little Cheshire cat-ish. Both eyes were skewed to one side; the photo was taken from a side angle, not straight on. Short hair, wavy and dark, topped his head. He had a big nose, no lumps or bumps, but wide, with large nostrils.

"What a schnoz on you." The oft said words of Louie, commenting on the size of my nose, came immediately to mind. Frequently compared to my mother's petite, perfectly straight nose, I was touchy about my larger appendage. Did I have Ernie's nose?

I wouldn't call Ernie handsome. Swarthy came to mind. My olive-toned complexion. He wore a white t-shirt under his wide-collared shirt, one button opened at his neck, the kind of shirt I imagined would be worn outside of his pants. Two-toned, the shirt had exaggerated, large stitches running vertically on each side, dividing the two hues. He had big ears, or a big ear, since I could see only one side of his head.

I set the photograph an arms-length away, picked up the copy of Ernie's death certificate. "Occlusive atherosclerosis of coronary arteries" was the cause of death. He was pronounced dead at noon, in the Village of Port Chester in Westchester County, New York on November 12, 1969. One day before my eighteenth birthday, I realized. Google told me it was a Wednesday. Was I attending a class at my community college when he died? Having lunch?

The copy of my grandmother's birth certificate, or "Certificato Di Nascita", as it was written in Italian, showed the creases and discoloration of a fragile, worn document. A typed form, the empty spaces for names and dates were filled in with florid handwriting. Angiolina Apicella was born May 6, 1890 in the town of Maiori, the province of Salerno, Italy. A quick Google search told me Maiori was less than two-and-a-half miles south of Amalfi on the famed Amalfi coast, a destination on my bucket-list for decades.

My mother, sister and I had visited Genoa, Rome and Florence, Italy the year I graduated from high school. What was it like for my mother to keep my ancestry secret during our trip?

I had a million questions and no answers. Did Louie and Ernie know each other? Both men were in the merchant marine, worked on ships, and were in and out of the same union hall in New York during the same time period. Nick ran a search on which ships they disembarked from in New York to see if they were ever on the same ship. They weren't. In his final report on my search, Nick had concluded that "it appears that they ran in the same circles and may have even known each other".

I was pulled to the conclusion that they did meet at some point. Louie's accusations of my mental illness led me to think Louie met Ernie, didn't like him, and branded him "mentally ill", and deduced that I, as his progeny, was mentally ill as well. It wouldn't have been the first time Louie made that leap in judgement. After arguments with his sister, a long-time friend and also a next-door neighbor, Louie made the same pronouncement about their mental health. Of course, I'd never know for sure if I were correct. Just one of many mysteries I'd never solve. But it was satisfying to juggle the puzzle pieces, to have a plausible reason to explain Louie's harsh assessment of my mental health and the arms-length distance he kept between us.

Chapter 19

When I was in my early fifties I traveled to Latvia to visit Riga, to root my mother's memories in the concrete setting of her birthplace. I had the tape recordings I'd made of her with me and listened to stories about her life in Riga as I toured the city.

"After my father died, his sister, a spinster, she was a dietitian at the hospital in Riga, a rarity for a woman at that time," my mother's voice, continuing her story during our walk months before in La Jolla, now spoke in my ear as I stood in front of the Riga opera house. "She had money, and sometimes she'd bring us books, and if we were really lucky, she'd take us to the opera, an unimaginable luxury. I loved it."

I imagined my mother, braided pigtails flying behind her, skipping through the flower maze on the lawn in front of the ionic columns of the ornate, white-stone opera house on the bank of the Riga canal.

As I took my seat inside the famed hall, excited to see Puccini's opera Turandot, I imagined my mother as a child, perched on the red velour seat next to me, her feet dangling above the floor, pumping to and fro, her head leaned back, mouth agape, awed by the domed gold ceiling, its crystal chandelier reflected in her hazel eyes. Barely containing her excitement, her head swiveled around to see the gold frescos of thespian masks and lutes adorning the porticos. I wondered if she'd wished she could wrap herself in the lush, magenta velour stage curtains like I wished I could.

The next day I walked the narrow cobblestone streets of old Riga, ornate buildings painted in rose and yellows, their trellises laden with verdant green ivies. The city was abuzz with summer solstice festivities. "Ligo, my favorite time of the year," my mother whispered in my ear. I imagined her among the group of school children, the girls in short orange-plaid skirts, white blouses, green vests, the boys in white shorts and red vests. The girls had red and green ribbons braided into their hair, the braids coiled around each ear. Encircled atop their heads were tapestried bands of red, green and white. The kids chattered among themselves, their steps bounced with excitement as they swarmed Riga's central square, prepared to dance around the Maypole, adorned with flowers. Was my mother once this carefree?

Before I'd left on the trip, my mother had told me of her high school in Riga, now the Art Academy of Latvia, a beautiful neo-gothic brick building in a park near the National Museum of Art. "I was good at math," my mother would often boast. I imagined her pushing open the glossy, heavy wooden doors, books and papers cradled under one arm. I knew her dreams of becoming a mathematician were exploded when the Russians invaded Latvia in 1944 and she and her mother joined the river of refugees fleeing the violence. "I kept my algebra notes, my trigonometry notes, the whole time we were in the camps," she'd said. "When the war was over, the Americans and English were organizing refugee camps. Boys who had survived the war were coming back and schools were organized. Right away I became a teacher. I still had my math notes and I was teaching boys who were much older than I was."

The solidity of the brick school building made palpable the disappointment my mother must have felt when she had to abandon her career dreams during the war. She was never able to resume her goals in the United States, although, in her fifties she took a secretarial job at a hospital and, in several years, rose to become the head auditor in charge of hospital finances, a position of which she was very proud. As a child, I'd bristled when she would berate me about my lack of comprehension of advanced math concepts. "If only you'd inherited my brain," she'd said more than once, shoving my homework across the kitchen table and stomping off in a huff. But standing in front of the origin of her dreams, I realized her irritation was most likely more a reliving of her own disappointment and less a condemnation of me.

Later that day, I looked up the address of my mother and grandmother's apartment. Away from the upscale and ornate old town, the street was nondescript, the three-story building unadorned. A well-worn rectangular stone, a step-up to the doorway, caught my eye.

"I was anxious even as a child," my mother had confessed to me once in a rare moment of self-disclosure. "I used to sit on the stoop of our apartment building in Riga, my stomach in knots, twisting my braids. What I was afraid of, I don't remember." I knelt and rested my hand on the cool stone, wished I could comfort the little girl twisting her braid. I wondered if her anxiety fueled the demanding, controlling behavior of the adult she'd become.

In preparation for my trip I'd read up on Latvian history. A small country on the Baltic Sea, between Lithuania and Estonia, Latvia has a tumultuous past. Before 1918, when the territory declared independence from Germany and became the Republic of Latvia, the area had been, for centuries, a battlefield of many devastating wars and the target of many conquerors vying for its location as a major east-west and north-south crossroads. In the late 19th century, a continuous German presence influenced the culture of the area. Spurred by the inspiration of the 1905 Revolution in Russia, Latvians revolted against the German ruling class and won independence. But during WWI Germany and Russia again fought for control of Latvia, creating a diaspora of refugees.

In 1940, near the onset of WWII, Latvia was occupied by the USSR and declared a republic of the Soviet Union, sparking a resistance movement to counter unwanted influence in the political, cultural and religious life of the people. My mother was fifteen at the time.

"All of a sudden everything at school was taught in Russian," she'd told me once. "We weren't even allowed to speak Latvian in class."

Who's My Daddy?

Large-scale deportations from Latvia to distant regions in the Soviet Union, mostly of families with leading positions in state and local governments, economy and culture, began in early June of 1941. By late June, Nazi Germany attacked Riga, and a week later Latvia was in German hands.

"Now everything was taught in German," my mother said. "Luckily, I was good at languages. I spoke Polish, my mother's native tongue, Latvian, Russian and German. I think it made learning English, when the time came, easier."

As in other Nazi-occupied countries, people in positions of leadership of the police and local governments were pressured to collaborate with the Nazis and form "self-defense units" to rid their country of communist functionaries and activists. Approximately 6,000 communists were killed. The Holocaust against Latvian Jews and the Roma began in July of 1941. Jews were ordered shot in Riga and many smaller towns or were forced into a ghetto in the Riga suburbs. By December of 1941, approximately 70,000 Latvian Jews were annihilated. Thousands of others, including Jews from other countries, were put into concentration camps, the largest of which was located in Riga.

"My mother was Catholic, so I was, too. We weren't really aware of what exactly what was going on," my mother had told me. "I remember seeing barbed wire in certain neighborhoods. I remember seeing 'Jewish swine' written in white paint on a store window. I remember a neighbor being led away by the police. But mostly we were busy trying to find enough food to feed ourselves. I was in school still. And my mother was constantly worried about my brother Peter in the army. When we finally heard he'd been killed in some battle somewhere, she went to pieces."

The Soviet Red Army again invaded Latvia in June of 1944, and by October they controlled the capital, Riga.

I thought of this history and what my mother had told me as I stood on the banks of the Daugava River, which connects Riga, Latvia's capital, with the Baltic Sea, the gateway to the rest of Europe. She'd said its docks were where refugees had boarded ships to leave the country during the war. At a latitude of 57 degrees, Riga's sky seemed to be higher in the atmosphere than cities in the US. The clouds seemed farther away in the expansive, vast blue sky. Chilly for a summer day, the leaves on the surrounding trees shimmered with lingering moisture from a morning downpour. I turned on my tape recorder, held it close to my ear and listened to my mother's voice.

"It was 1944, October, in Riga, and we were surrounded by Russian troops. There were horror stories being told about what the Russian soldiers were doing to the women and children - killing them, the same thing that the Germans were doing. But just more awful, so you were listening to that stuff and you wanted to get out and run away. Because you were alive. We gathered up whatever we could and mainly what I was saving were my books, my school books, because I had just finished school. I was going to enter the university. We called a horse and buggy and they put your stuff in the buggy and took you to the docks and if there was a ship available you just got on it. Wherever it went you went with the ship. It wasn't like a cruise ship with cabins and all that. They helped you carry on your stuff and there was some straw in the hull and you spread your blanket and that was your spot with hundreds of other people on that ship. That voyage, I don't remember. It is like in a fog. I know we sailed to Danzig that used to belong to Poland, but now the Germans had taken it over."

I had never understood, nor had my mother been able to explain to me, why refugees from the Baltic countries, after the Soviet invasion, had been relocated to Nazi Germany. It seemed counter-intuitive to me. I visited the Museum of the Occupation of Latvia, housed in a Soviet-era style blocky building, incongruous in the old historic city center of Riga, to learn more.

My guide, Peter, was a young man, dark haired and fair-skinned, like many I'd seen the day before at the summer solstice festivities, decked out with leafy green wreaths on their heads. We stood in a chilly hall echoing the footsteps of other tourists, looking at old black and white photos of Riga from the 1940's.

"It took a while for the USSR to gain control," Peter, speaking excellent English, answered my question about Latvian migration to Germany. "And during that time the German authorities began evacuating civilians from Latvia to Germany, so as to leave as few people as possible behind for the enemy and to use evacuees to put more workers into the German labor pool, which had lost thousands."

He pointed me to a chart delineating the migration out of Latvia during WWII. Approximately 150,000 people left in the final phase of the war, my mother and grandmother among them. In addition, if you include all the people either deported, killed, or victims of the Holocaust, some historians calculate that Latvia's population decreased 70% by war's end.

Peter was interested in my mother's refugee experience. He pointed out photos of refugees awaiting ships on the docks of the Dauvaga River where I had stood that morning. I imagined my mother and grandmother, bundled up against the cold October air, among the crowd.

"My mother insisted on bringing her Singer sewing machine," my mother had told me many times. "We schlepped that crate with us on and off docks for years."

The sewing machine, its ornate black shiny base painted with flowers in gold filigree, had been taken off its foot-pedal base and put in a carrying case. Once in the US, my mother had it converted to an electric machine, and she'd sewn many outfits for me and my sister on that machine. When I tried my hand as seamstress in my early twenties, she bequeathed me the heirloom. During my nomadic twenties, in a move from the west to east coast, I asked a friend to store the Singer in his garage. But too many years had passed before I thought to retrieve it, and I'd never been able to find that friend. My mother, incensed by my carelessness, often reminded me of my transgression. Looking at the photos of refugees, huddled with their precious possessions, my eyes filled with tears and I was again seized with guilt and remorse at the loss of such an historic artifact.

Peter and I listened to my mother, on tape, recounting a story of the first displaced persons camp where she'd landed:

"After the ship docked in Germany we were put on a train. It stopped near big barracks, refugee barracks that were filled with all kind of refugees, Poles, Latvians, Lithuanians, Estonians, people from Denmark. It was a camp where they stored people who would work in German industry. They put us in huge barracks, and that means it's very cold. You had straw and each person got their little suitcases, laid them alongside the straw, and that was your little domain in there. The nights were, they were horrible because children cried and people coughed and the smell was, well, you can imagine a barracks of about maybe a hundred people. All kinds of classes, low class people that fought and cursed. You're stuck in there. There's nowhere to go, nowhere. And you lined up in the morning and they gave you food and then there were the barracks where you went to wash. My mother was beside herself completely. I just rolled with the punches. I was 18 years old, sort of numb and stupid. The Germans started showing propaganda movies, describing wonderful places where the boys and girls are in beautiful uniforms living in beautiful dormitories, doing wonderful work like taking care of children in daycare centers. They wanted us to join and showed us the marches and bonfires and singing we could have if we joined. I thought it was so wonderful and I wanted to join. I was no Nazi, I was no Communist, I was nothing. I was just a kid and I just wanted to get out of the camps. But I had my mother and she would have to stay alone. So you will never do that. You wouldn't leave her alone. So I couldn't go."

As I listened, I thought of my own life in my late teens. I'd moved across the country from my mother at nineteen, set out on my own independent journey. "Why did you have to go so far away?" she'd often scolded me. I'd inwardly bristled with a mixture of guilt and resentment at her insinuation that I wasn't living up to her expectations of a daughter. Yet, standing in the museum, amid the evidence of a war-torn people, hearing the sacrifices she made for her own mother, I realized how the constraints of her own youth must have chaffed against the free-spirited opportunities of mine.

"I've heard many stories like hers from my relatives," Peter said, bringing me back from my revere. "The wars and occupations left such a scar on the Latvian psyche. So much so that we built a whole museum in commemoration."

Peter's explanation of how the Nazis exploited refugee labor in Germany fit with my mother's experiences. I flipped the tape cassette to begin side two and Peter and I bent our heads together to catch my mother's words.

"The Germans at that first camp started announcing different job opportunities. I met a woman about 30 who was also with her mother. We decided to stick together. The Germans were looking for factory workers in a torpedo factory. They had a hidden factory in the woods and my friend and I went. They asked me about my education and selected me to work in a personnel office.

"When I got the job they transferred me and my mother to another camp, different barracks. Here we had bunk beds and a little steel closet, so it was a little more civilized. The camp was near the factory and I had to walk through the woods because everything was camouflaged.

"Every morning I walked to the torpedo factory. Battalions were watching the sky for planes. If they heard Russian planes they released an artificial fog to cover the whole area so the bombers couldn't see where the factory was. If you happened to walk when they released it, you inhaled the stuff and it fell on your skin. They said it wasn't dangerous, who knows?

"I started working there the beginning of November in 1944. The main boss was some kind of German nobility and he had two sons that had died fighting in Latvia when the Germans invaded Latvia in 1941. He was very nice to me. I still have a certificate he gave me when we were leaving, when the war was almost over and the Germans were running away. He gave me a certificate for good performance. I was a very good employee.

"My immediate boss, the personnel director, was a real Nazi, with insignias everywhere. He was nice to me too, sharing his lunch and sandwiches. I did translation because I spoke Latvian and Russian and German, so my boss would call me to translate for him. Many a time people didn't get to hear what he was really saying, because that good I wasn't. I must have been smart, but manipulative, because I'd just say anything. So we laughed a lot.

"One cold night I didn't have any shoes and they gave me real army boots up to my knees and an army coat and a bicycle. I pedaled around the place. The area was very pretty, very well kept. I went back to the barracks at night to eat. We had meat once a week, Sundays, a funny meat that was like shoe leather, always with a floury gravy. The gravy was full of little maggots, so we pushed those away. I laughed about it. When you are a kid, you develop a different attitude than your parent. My mother was constantly worried, constantly wondering what will happen to you. But we kids, we would sit on top of a table, a big table in the middle of the barracks, and this boy had a harmonica and he played all the songs and we sang and it was like communal living."

"Your mother kept a sunny spirit during a really difficult time," Peter remarked when I shut off the tape recorder. "She seems like a strong person."

"My sister and I often marvel about our mom's strong backbone and good sense of humor," I agreed. I didn't say what I was really thinking, that often her outward demeanor seemed like a façade, a cover-up for deeper, more troubled, feelings.

I thanked Peter for his attention and expertise and left the museum, vowing, upon my return to the US, to ask my mother more about the pivotal experiences that had shaped her sense of self and influenced her personality. Perhaps I could uncover more about what was beneath our difficult relationship.

Chapter 20

In May, one year after I found out Louie wasn't my biological father, Walter and I took the Hudson Line north out of Manhattan's Grand Central Station to New Rochelle, New York, to meet my Italian first cousins. Carol and her sister Angela were picking us up at the train station at 12:10 pm. We left Brooklyn under a monotonous metallic grey sky, bundled up in down jackets and hats to ward off the cold, blustery un-spring-like day, clomped down the subway entrance, and swiped our metro passes to push through the turnstyle to the F train. The screech of the subway train's wheels on the metal tracks matched the pitch of my jangled nerves, taut with anxiety over the impending visit. We grabbed for the handrails as our train car lurched forward, found seats and settled in for the first leg of the journey.

We'd been cat and house sitting at my sister and brother-in-law's home in Brooklyn, having seen them off on a trip to Europe, and spent the last few days wandering a Joan Miro exhibit at the Museum of Modern Art, catching the updated version of Oklahoma on Broadway, and doing what one does in New York City – walk, walk, walk for miles. Walter and I had met, and lived together, in Manhattan thirty-eight years before. We'd returned as tourists many times over the last decades with our list of nostalgic must-dos – cannoli at Veniero's Italian Bakery in the Lower East Side, egg cream at the B & H Dairy around the corner, smoked mozzarella cheese at a deli in Greenwich Village - along with our favorite uptown museums. But this year, a thrumming anticipation accompanied my every step, kept me awake at night. I was meeting my biological father's family!

I had carefully selected a bottle of Flora-Falanghina Beneventano, a white wine, from grapes grown in a vineyard in the province, Salerno, where our grandparents had lived in Italy, as a hostess gift. Just as carefully, I'd picked out my outfit – not too dressy, not too casual – a black, long-sleeved tunic over tights, a variegated pink and tan silk scarf as accent, emerald-green earrings I'd bought from a street vendor near the wine store, and my favorite ankle boots. No matter how carefully I'd planned to get a good night's rest, sleep was elusive, even with a prescription sleeping pill. Instead, my eyes popped open at 2:30 am. I was stretched out on the bed in my sister's spare room, now strewn with my suitcase and clothes, two tall windows facing the street, the sheer curtains lit by an outside orb. Was it a full moon? Could I count on Luna's glow to light my path? A peek through the curtains revealed only a streetlamp. I was on my own. Not true. Walter, with his calm, supportive presence, was beside me.

Today was the crescendo of the last twelve months, all the delving and revelations. Today I was meeting the family that would have been mine – the life I would have had, the foundation, the connections, the people who would have been at my birthday parties, graduations and wedding, and I at theirs. All the small talk around the lunch table, the Thanksgivings and Christmases, all of it a different life, another world from the one I'd had. My body knew what a huge day today was, regardless of my mind's instruction to "be calm, go back to sleep", as if Ernie's DNA inside me was vibrating at peak intensity now, the twisted strands straining to spark an electric arc to our family roots. I was excited. And hopeful. And scared. I wondered how my Italian cousins felt. I had offered to Uber from the train station to Angela's house. Are they picking us up at the station to avoid giving us her address, in case we're fraudsters?

*

Several evenings before, I had joined my Markowitz cousins, Louie's nephews and niece, for a different family reunion.

"Will you have a new revelation for me this year?" I teased Dan. He had confessed he often regretted spilling the beans about my father at last year's reunion, which was exactly one year ago to the day.

"I didn't mean to upset your life," he said.

"I'm so grateful you told me," I said. "The truth explains so many of those hard-to-explain undercurrents I'd always felt in my family. It's a relief to know I wasn't just imagining the tension."

"How has this past year been for you?" Linda, my cousin's wife and a psychotherapist, asked as she and my sister Vicki joined us around the dinner table.

"I think I was in shock for the first four or five months," I said. "Nauseous a lot, walking around in a fog. That lessened as the year went on, but now, having just read the genealogist's report, the hard evidence confirming the lies, I'm back to nauseous again."

"You've had a deep trauma," Linda said with gravitas.

Trauma. The word reverberated through my body. Trauma was serious. I had never associated trauma with my situation. The gravity of Linda's words, backed by her experience as a therapist, her kind and concerned eyes as she said them, brought on my tears and a hot flash. I'd had a deep trauma. There it was. Spoken out loud. Said as fact. Heard by my sister. A dinner napkin caught my tears, the room receded. And then the waves passed, and I heard Vicki describe our mother's delusions of grandeur, her narcissism.

"She should have been born into a royal family, born a queen," Vicki said.

"How is it you both function so well in the world?" Linda asked Vicki and me. "With all your histories?"

"Lots of therapy," I said. Vicki just shrugged, and raised her wine glass in mock salute.

"The hardest thing for me," Vicki said, "Is the deception. The lies."

"Both of you experienced trauma," Linda said. I realized that, yes, Vicki had, too. In a different way than I had, but trauma nevertheless. We just had different ways of dealing with it. After all, she was six years younger than I, so she had watched me, and our parents' reactions to me, and learned what not to do to get along, to escape the rejection I'd felt. She learned different coping strategies, was so much better at deflecting and subverting her feelings than I.

Several months after I'd found out Louie wasn't my real father, my sister and I met for brunch when she was in Los Angeles on a work assignment. The recent family revelations were on both our minds.

"When I was a little kid, I often felt like I'd been born into the wrong family," my sister confided. "I remember sitting at the breakfast table when I was five years old. I looked around and thought 'who are these people?'" She'd been looking at Louie, our mother and me. "I thought 'how dare these adults tell me what to do? They're not really my parents'."

At the time of our brunch, I'd asked questions, tried to probe deeper into my sister's feelings. She'd cracked a joke and moved on to a lighter topic, as she was apt to do whenever our conversation got too personal. I was left perplexed by her disclosure. After all, I was the child who didn't belong to one of the parents at the table. I had always felt a deep disconnect between Louie and myself, felt that something was "off" in our family. Now, looking through the lens of family trauma, I wondered if my sister, as a young child, had tried to make sense of the secrecy swirling around our family home. Had she overheard a conversation between Louie and our mother? Had she somehow intuited that someone didn't belong at the breakfast table, and then made the story about herself, as children are apt to do? Both she and I were left feeling that we didn't belong. Both of us suffered from the secrets and lies endemic in our childhood home.

"Next stop, Broadway and Lafayette," the conductor announced over the subway's speakers, jolting me out of my thoughts. Walter and I bumped shoulders with fellow passengers, hustling out of the train car to navigate the escalators and tunnels of the underground maze to transfer to the six-train and Grand Central Station, one step closer to my Italian family.

Chapter 21

Walter and I exited the train at the New Rochelle station on an outdoor platform, the wind whipping our coats open. A flat grey sky muted the contour and color of the surrounding suburban neighborhood. The guardrails were rusty, the concrete egress winding down from the platform to the street cracked and uneven. We had to watch our step. We spotted a car and a few taxis on the street below. At first, I didn't see anyone who looked like my cousin Carol. Then a car passenger door opened and a woman with salt and pepper hair stepped out and waved her arms in the air. I returned her gesture and floated over the next few hundred feet.

"Is it really you?" my cousin Carol said, her voice a high octave. I stopped a couple of feet in front of her, the Carol of our FaceTime call, laugh lines etched around her eyes, watery with tears. She opened her arms.

"I feel like I've been waiting forever to meet you," Carol said. We each took a half-step forward. I flipped the tote bag hanging at my side behind me, and all but collapsed into Carol's hug.

"My sister, Angela," Carol said as we pulled apart, accenting the second syllable of the name. Angela, younger than Carol, had dark brown hair and a stocky build. Her brown eyes shifted away from mine quickly, her hug was brief. Had I read wariness there?

Walter stood near Carol, chatting. Would a passing motorist take us for a family?

*

We arrived at Angela's home just as a car pulled up.

"Our sister, Debbie, the youngest." Carol said.

Debbie was slender, in jeans and a pink top, with long brown hair, in her fifties. She bounded up the walkway with my long-legged lope. Her skin color was exactly mine, olive, but not just olive, exactly the same olive hue as mine. Our faces, although not the same oval, had the same high forehead and cheekbones.

"You're right," Debbie nodded at Carol and Angela. "Gina and I do look like sisters."

"For you," Carol said as she handed me a pink and white polka dot gift bag after we'd shrugged off our coats inside Angela's front room. I felt Carol's eyes on my face as I opened the bag and pulled out an 8 X 10 framed black and white photograph of a young man, sailor hat atop wavy hair, a young man with a toothy grin. He had exactly my eyes, their shape, the distance between them, the angle at which my eyelid fell over the iris. A jolt of recognition, a kinship, surged up my spine.

"It's him?" I gasped. This man looked very different from the older man in the photo Carol had emailed me.

"Yes, it's Ernie, your father." Carol took a step toward me.

"Do you think he knew about me?" I asked, choking back tears.

"We don't know," Carol said. "You're a complete surprise to us."

I had worried we'd be awkward with each other. Instead, we sat around Angela's kitchen table and talk flowed easily over a lunch platter replete with rolled ham and salami, pickled artichokes, olives, hummus and crackers. I loaded up my plate, suddenly ravenously hungry.

At my prompting, my cousins told me about the life I would have lived had I been raised a Ferrino: all the kids went to St. Joseph's parochial school from first to twelfth grade; the adults had working class jobs; everyone loved to play cards. My cousins' mother Fanny went to church every morning at eight o'clock.

"My mother's recipe," Carol said, flourishing a sour cream coffee cake she'd baked that morning.

"She made this same cake for all the big family gatherings," Carol said as we all oohed and aahed over the delicious confection. "All of us, aunts, uncles, cousins, we were together every weekend, all the holidays. My house was the meeting spot. The minute someone would walk through the door my mother would hand them a bowl of meatballs."

So different than the small nuclear family I grew up in, I thought, just the four of us, a thousand miles from any relatives.

My cousins described my father as a fun-loving guy, caring, always kind, quick to lend a hand. He drove a Mustang. Mr. Chips, his cocker spaniel, was a constant companion.

Ernie sounds like the complete opposite of Louie, I thought.

"He lived with a woman for a while, didn't he?" Angela, clearing dishes off the table, asked her sisters.

"Thelma," Carol said. "That would've been after Gina was born, later in the 1950s. He wouldn't marry her and she left him."

Unusual for a guy from a Catholic background, I thought. And not for the first time I wondered if Ernie was gay, or bisexual, trying out the heterosexual life, deciding it was not for him. Was that why he and my mother had parted? Why he never married?

"When you were growing up," Carol spoke slowly and looked down at her placemat as she curled and uncurled its edge with her fingers, "did you feel a difference in how your father treated you versus your sister?" She raised her head and looked into my eyes.

Taken aback by her question, I stammered. I had made a decision days before not to divulge my estrangement from Louie, not to expose that painful chapter in my history during this first meeting with my cousins. But this question went even deeper.

"I found an old home movie a few months ago," Walter said. He put down his fork and pushed back his chair. "Louie shot a scene at a park with his super 8. It looked like Gina was about nine. Vicki would have been three?" He looked at me for confirmation. I nodded.

"The thing that struck me," Walter continued, "was the difference of how long Louie focused the camera on one daughter, then the other, as they ran around. It was really obvious. Gina would be on for a second or two, then he'd focus on Vicki for a much longer. I got really distracted once I noticed. It went back and forth like that for the whole movie."

I was red with embarrassment at the insinuation in Walter's story that my father felt a preference for his youngest daughter. I had never wanted to fall prey to feeling less cared for than my sister. Sibling rivalry for a parent's affection was common, I knew from my background in psychology. And Louie wasn't all warm and fuzzy with Vicki either. I hadn't wanted to fan flames of victimhood in myself. But had I felt a difference? Yes. I blamed myself. I wasn't as light-spirited as my sister was, not as facile with a funny story. Of course, he'd like her more. When he agreed to send Vicki to a four-year college, after I, a National Honor Student in high school, begged to go but was told the local community college was all I was going to get, I was confused. Why hadn't I been able to go?

Just the fact that I'd felt the difference caused me shame. I heard my mother's voice, "She's your younger sister, you should take care of her. You're so selfish". I should celebrate my sister's advantages, not compare myself to her.

I had internalized my mother's accusations that jealousy was a stain on my character, not to be admitted, a shame to be hidden away.

Yet here was the obvious question, now that the truth was out that I wasn't Louie's offspring. Carol was the first person, aside from my husband, to open the door to my feelings.

"Yes, I did feel a difference," I finally said. "I always tried not to blow it out of proportion."

"Now you know you weren't crazy to feel that." Carol leaned forward, reached out a hand to me.

I bathed in her words and gesture - a simple acknowledgement of my perceptions, believed as fact, no judgement. Seen, and accepted, I felt more and more at home.

*

The aroma of garlic and oregano greeted us at the Villagio Ristorante & Pizzeria, where my cousin Linda D., who I'd not yet met, was already seated and awaiting our arrival for dinner.

 Without Linda, it would have taken much longer to locate my Italian family. Her DNA had first identified me as a Ferrino. Tall, with her frosted hair swept in an up-do, Linda sat with her shoulders erect. She greeted me warmly but didn't join in the banter of the sisters as our waiter laid our table and we dug into the antipastos, pastas and pizza.

"Do you see the people coming across the border?" Linda, next to me, suddenly asked in a quiet voice. Building a wall between the US and Mexico had been a major topic in the recent news.

"No." I explained that San Diego was three cities north of the Mexican border, too far to witness any migration. "It's sad," I began again. "The immigrants are trying to…," and paused.

"Get all the free stuff here," Carol said from across the table.

"Get jobs to support their families," I said at the same time. Carol turned her head quickly, looking away. I felt my first flash of discord that day. Donald Trump had been president for over two years. Political disagreement was rife. I realized my cousin Carol and I had a basic disagreement on a subject dear to my heart.

That brief instant gave me a lot to ponder in the next months. Carol was so warm and welcoming to me, a virtual stranger. Why didn't she extend that open-heartedness to other people? Was it only because she and I shared the same blood? Hadn't our grandparents been immigrants, searching for a better life? Italian immigrants had suffered disdain and humiliation on US soil for decades. Why didn't Carol make the connection between her roots and the plight of newly arriving migrants? And why did I?

*

Walter and I leaned against each other's shoulder on the train back to Manhattan, sharing photos we'd taken during the day on our cell phones, exchanging thoughts about the hours spent with my new relatives. We'd parted from my cousins with bear hugs and vows to stay in touch, to meet again soon.

"No denying the family resemblance," Walter said. In the photo on his phone, I'm holding up Carol's coffee cake, surrounded by my cousins, each of us grinning ear to ear. What exactly was it about our likeness? Hard to define. I just seemed to fit in.

In another photo, Carol and I are at the cemetery of the Holy Sepulchre. We had made a special trip there to see Ernie's grave on our way to the Italian restaurant. The sky was blown-out white, the sugar maple trees leafed with the light green of new spring growth. We were surrounded by row after row of tombstones, irregularly spaced, among the thick, coarse grass. Each of us had a hand atop opposite sides of a granite headstone. I had never before stood in the cemetery of my ancestors. My mother and Louie had been cremated; Louie's ashes scattered over the ocean, my mother's ashes still in a closet in my garage. The headstone felt warm under my hand. I was surprised to find myself shaken by the thought that some fragment of my father existed beneath my feet.

I enlarged the screen on the cell phone with my fingers. "St. Anthony Pray for Us" was carved below the name, "Ferrigno", the original spelling of Ferrino, preferred by our grandfather. Above those words, there was a detailed carving of St. Anthony, eyes downcast, lips pursed as if to speak comforting words to the small child he cradled in his arms. The sides of the tombstone were carved with lilies. Ernie and his mother were buried with Ernie's brother Joseph and his wife, and their names and dates of birth and death were listed under the word "Beloved" for each.

"One day Ernie told my mother he had a pain in his left arm," Carol had said, her hair a halo, backlit by the diffuse light. "But what did we know back then?" She'd grimaced.

"Next day he had a massive heart attack. My mother always felt bad about that."

Next, Walter held up a photo of a monolithic brown brick building. Angela had stopped the car in front of it on our way to the restaurant.

"Up there," Carol had stuck her arm out the window, pointing a finger. "Fourth floor, on the left there, the one with the fan in the window," she'd said. "Ernie lived in that apartment for the last several years before he died."

I'd imagined my father sitting on his window ledge surveying the shops across the street. I'd breathed deep, envisaged molecules exhaled from Ernie's lungs recirculating in and out, in and out of the lungs of this neighborhood's denizens over the decades. Could I breathe a piece of Ernie in here on this street? Make him corporeal in my body?

The train rumbled to a stop. We arrived at Grand Central Station and wound our way past bagel shops, florists and pretzel stands to find the subway to our Brooklyn home for one more night before returning to San Diego and normal life.

Chapter 22

Once I was home from New York, texts flew back and forth between my cousins and me. We connected on Facebook. A bouquet of flowers arrived at my door. "We welcome you with love to our family" the card read.

I'd found my lovely new family. I should have felt happy but I couldn't shake my lethargy. I felt heavy, my head stuffed with cotton.

A sense of dislocation, like being above the sea with a scuba tank on, or below it without one, accompanied me. Either way, I struggled to breathe deeply.

All the anticipation of the trip – the unknown, the hesitancy, the mystery – was past. Now I had answers. Did I feel let down? No, that wasn't it. I had a body sense of fading, as if my right hand, reaching for my left arm, might pass right through flesh, skin and bone. Now that I knew what my life as a Ferrino might have been – the truncated possibility of that life hummed on some sort of cellular level, mitochondria never quite evolved, pulsating faintly. A wisp of smoke. Steam from a subway grate on 42nd Street in Manhattan. What difference does it all make? Get over it. The thought nagged at me.

*

"I'm Gina," I said to the older gentleman sitting next to me at the carwash, returning his handshake. Back in the routines of daily life, I'd been home from New York for several weeks.

"Ah, like Gina Lollobrigida," he smiled.

"Obviously not," I smirked. "But I am Italian."

"What's your family name?" he asked.

"Ferrino," popped out of my mouth.

"How do you spell that?" he wanted to know.

I told him, matter of fact. No description of the upheaval of the last months, no nature vs nurture debate, not even a mention of my mixed heritage. I blithely claimed my Italian roots for the first time.

Mom would be furious with me, I thought, driving to the Y. Furious I'd found out, furious I'd claimed his name. She never wanted me to know.

"How dare you?" I heard her shrill voice. "You should be ashamed of yourself."

Bile rose in my throat. Guilty. I'd betrayed her. She'd be very unhappy.

I pounded out laps in the pool, free-style, back-stroke, back and forth, over and over, trying to focus on my breathing, trying to shut off the accusing voice of my mother in my head. I'd stopped to catch my breath, my hand on the rough concrete of the pool's edge, when struck by a jolting thought: I was holding onto pain and grief because my mother didn't want me to know the truth she'd guarded since my birth. She'd be angry I'd found out. I'd broken a covenant of secrecy. Daughters who disobey must suffer, suffer for making mommy sad and unhappy. I'd been making myself suffer to remain loyal to my mother; to show fealty. Long dead, she still exercised control in my head.

I'd learned the truth: Louie March was not my father, not my blood, not my DNA, and not a weight around my neck anymore. I no longer had to struggle to figure out why he was so chilly, so quick to throw me out of the house, to disown me. The truth was I wasn't his biological daughter and he didn't have the capacity to embrace me as his. That was never my fault. Finding out the truth had the power to free me of his condemnation once and for all. I didn't need to protect my mother from my right to exalt in these truths. I could shed the shame and blame and revel in my new-found freedom.

My body buoyant, I aced the remaining laps in my mile routine and popped out of the pool feeling light and cheery. It wasn't the first time a demanding physical workout had shaken loose the circuitry in my brain to create a novel solution to a problem. I didn't understand the neurochemistry of the magic behind my realization, but I felt gleefully grateful for my new insight and lift out of despair.

Chapter 23

The summer after I'd met my new Italian family, new light was shed on another family mystery. I got a phone call, out of the blue, from a guy claiming to be Louie's grandson. His name was Brad, and his father, Jerome, was the son Louie abandoned when Jerome was a toddler, the son from Louie's first marriage. Brad had researched his father's heritage through Ancestry.com and spent hours at the New York City library combing through old merchant marine records. He emailed me the PDF of a book he'd written about his father's genealogy. Documents identified me as Louie's wife's daughter, and Brad assumed I was Louie's biological daughter also. Oddly, my sister Vicki, Louie's actual daughter, hadn't shown up in his research.

Brad's father, Jerome, Louie's son, was eighty years old, a retired attorney living in Seattle, WA. So began another journey to weave more new-found relatives into my family. My sister Vicki was thrilled to have found her half-brother.

Seeing the two of them together left no doubt they are related.

Even though I am not biologically related to Jerome, I felt bonded to him through the trauma we both experienced at Louie's hands. Jerome was genetically related to Louie. I was raised by him. Which influence was greater – nature or nurture? Louie walked away from his first wife and two-year-old son, never to contact them again. Jerome described, in our phone conversations, the web of secrets, lies and heartbreak resulting from his father's actions. Louie disowned me in my forties. Both Jerome and I suffered from Louie's pattern of abandonment.

Pieces of the puzzle, possible reasons for Louie's behavior, came to light. Jerome's mother was of Scandinavian heritage, and worshipped at a Lutheran Church. Jerome assumed anti-Jewish sentiment, prevalent in her family and tight-knit community, was the reason Louie left town. We will never know the whole story, but it seems highly probable anti-Semitism played at least a part in his decision. He had already changed his name from Markowitz to March before marrying his first wife. He must have been acutely sensitive to and aware of the anti-Jewish currents around him. Did his sensitivity to slights bolster a defensiveness in him, make him prone to lash out in anger? Was it easier, safer for him to abandon people than work out differences? Anti-Semitism could well be responsible for his flight response. Again, another example of how cultural and societal forces shaped the behavioral patterns of my parents, shaped their behavior towards me and shaped my own behavior.

Chapter 24

My mother and I debated her move from Florida into an "independent" living facility in San Diego for several years before she actually moved into one. Finally, when she was 82 years old and an episode of internal bleeding landed her in a hospital for several days, we both came face to face with her need to live close to family and help. My mother wasn't happy about the arrangement.

"An old age home," she'd sighed repeatedly. "Never thought I'd see the day. I took care of my mother until her dying day." Her meaning, not subtle in the least, was that it was my job to do the same for her.

On my end, I wasn't even sure I could handle having my mother in California, much less in my home. But, given our fractured history, the rebuilding we'd done since our four-year estrangement, I wanted to try. I still had the fantasy of having a close, open, relaxed relationship with my mother. Perhaps being together on a more consistent basis would allow that to happen. Close by, but not on top of each other every day. I also didn't want her to live nearby in an apartment without support, dependent on me for grocery shopping and, most of all, for constant companionship. I wanted to "put" her somewhere, somewhere not in my own home, somewhere else, not in my space every day. And I was plagued by the embarrassment and guilt those wants brought up. I was adopting the typical white, middle-class solution to caring for my aging parent. Putting her somewhere. What did that say about me?

My mother didn't hold back her opinion of my solution. "It's easy for you to care about the faceless hordes," my mother admonished me more than once when I'd express sympathy for victims of the global diaspora or other human beings facing hardship. "It's a lot harder to care for the people right in front of you," she'd follow up with a pointed stare. I hated to admit it, but she was right.

The Chateau La Jolla Inn, an independent living facility just minutes from my home, seemed a good compromise for both my mother and me. She'd have her own small apartment, meals provided in the dining room and the potential companionship of other residents, mostly women around her age. I'd have the privacy of the home my husband Walter and I shared yet be close enough to help out when needed.

My mother and I didn't, as was our pattern, ever openly hash out the real push and pull of why living together would be an unimaginable strain, on me, at least. In therapy, I worked on maintaining boundaries, on not taking the guilt bait, not getting triggered. I'd come a long way towards understanding my mother's controlling behavior as a result of her tumultuous history, the trauma of early deprivation and war. When she complained about "being institutionalized" I said "hmm, that's one way to look at things". I smiled a lot. I dodged. I snuck in comments on how small the house I lived in with Walter was. I deflected. I touted the benefits of the Chateau, it's walking proximity to the beach, to the shopping section of La Jolla, to the numerous activities provided by the staff, the classes and excursions. Neither of us fooled the other, but we struck an unspoken truce.

Chapter 25

"Your grandmother Natalia's handwork," my mother said as she unfolded a yellowed cloth, a yard long and five inches wide. We were emptying boxes moved from her condo in Florida to her new apartment in La Jolla, just minutes from my home in San Diego, where she'd moved when she was 83 years old.

On the cloth, the letters of the alphabet were embroidered in red thread, in twelve different fonts, down the length of the fabric. Precise, beautiful calligraphy, each letter a work of art.

"My mother was sent to a Polish convent as a young teenager," my mother said. "Her family couldn't afford to raise her. The nuns taught her to embroider and tat and she was expected to spend her days doing domestic tasks." My mother hands smoothed the wrinkled cloth. "She misbehaved and as punishment the nuns made her sit on the roof of the convent, in the cold winter, with her feet in a bucket of cold water. She had to sit there and make this tapestry." She looked me in the eye, the corners of her mouth in a deep frown.

"Jeeze," I said through my teeth. "So harsh. How'd she get out of the convent?"

"Somehow my father found her there, I'm not sure exactly how that happened. He married her and brought her to Latvia. Times were tough then." She shot me a glance. "You," she drew out the syllable as she lifted her eyebrows, twisted her lips and, with a quick downward peck of her jaw, said "you have no idea."

I felt the familiar jab of that "you", the accusation of how privileged my life was, how much suffering laid the path to my life of luxury. There was a subtext I couldn't quite grasp, that I'd somehow been responsible for the suffering, if only I'd admit it. Was I crazy to feel that?

My mother's shoulders slumped. She laid the tapestry aside. Her eyes sought out a corner of the room. The air felt heavy, as if the barometric pressure had skyrocketed. Why did we so often end up in this uncomfortable impasse?

I picked up the embroidered cloth, ran my fingers over the raised letters, imagined young Natalia plying her needle and red thread. I had only seen one sepia photo of her, remembered her face, unsmiling, full-lipped, the same classic high cheekbones as my mother, with her dark hair parted down the middle and drawn back. A serious young woman.

"Can I have Natalia's embroidery?" I said after a few moments of silence.

"Don't lose it this time," my mother said with a searing glance my way. Her meaning needed no explanation. She was referring to the old Singer sewing machine she and her mother had painstakingly carted from Riga, to numerous displaced persons camps during and after the war, and finally on the refugee ship to the U.S. The sewing machine I'd lost after she had bequeathed it to me. A transgression I'd never be allowed to forget. Without meeting my mother's eyes, I folded the cloth and placed it in my purse.

*

My mother didn't often speak of her mother or their relationship. When she did, it was matter-of-factly, without warmth or longing. "She was my mother and she expected me to take care of her," she'd say. "She was very demanding. You think I'm a problem…you should have had my mother."

When I returned home from my mother's apartment I dug up the manila folder with transcripts of the stories about WWII and the years immediately afterward, the ones my mother told me on our many walks together years before. I remembered she'd described her mother as "lace-curtain Polish" and I scanned the pages for the meaning of the term.

"My mother, was lace-curtain Polish," I read her words. "You've heard of lace-curtain Irish? Poor Irish immigrants who managed to move up in social status, put up lace curtains in their new kitchens? Well, my mother was lace-curtain Polish. She thought she was a lady, special. She just couldn't stand the conditions at the camps." My mother had been telling me about the displaced-persons camps her and her mother fled to during WWII.

"I was still working at the torpedo factory," I continued to read the transcript. "Things were getting worse in the camps. They were giving us less and less food. The Russians were coming closer and the war was going bad for the Germans. I'll never forget the day, March 14, 1945. My boss would give me his kidney-shaped metal dish every day before lunch and I would take it to the commissary and fill it up with soup. So that day, it was five minutes to twelve, and I got on the bike to pedal to the kitchen and the alarm started, and maybe two seconds after the alarm started the bombs started to fall. I dropped my bike near a hatch that covered these holes in the ground that were shelters. I pulled up the hatch and got into the hole. There was room for two or three people. A few minutes later, the hatch opened and somebody else got in there. There were explosions all over. They went on for maybe a half hour. We were crouched in that hole not knowing if we were going to get out alive. It quieted down, so we lifted the hatch up and ran further to where we knew there was a bigger bunker. I slid in. The walls were thicker there. We sat there and the explosions lasted for another half hour and then quieted down.

"We got out, and it was unreal, absolutely unreal. Fires all around. People running in different directions. I don't remember much. I just don't. I didn't know what was happening in the camp. I didn't know if my mother was alive. I didn't know where to run because of the fires and the bomb craters. It was pandemonium. Finally, we did find each other. Somebody had told my mother that they saw my dead body somewhere. You can imagine how she was when we saw each other."

My eyes filled with tears and blurred the letters on the page. I could only imagine the horror of thinking your daughter, or your mother, was dead under a bomb. The possibility sent a wave of nausea up my throat. Even though several years had passed since my mother had told me the story, I remembered the telling well. We'd been walking the shoreline of the La Jolla coast, me on my mother's left side, hands clasped, elbows at our waistline, our bodies close together. Our usual walking posture. She'd held a dictaphone in her right hand. I'd had to repeatedly urge her to keep the dictaphone near her mouth. The surface of the sea danced with light reflected from a bright blue sky, belying the darkness of the history being shared.

I'd been worried that the telling was taking too much of a toll on my mother. She'd picked up the pace of our steps and her words had taken on a rote, chopped cadence.

"Let's take a break," I'd said. "A break from remembering all this. Are you tired?"

"No, I want to get it over with," she'd stopped walking, turned to face me and said, "The past is the past. The inhumanity still goes on." Her voice took on a didactic tone. "Just watch the news on TV. More wars. Nothing changes. It's what people have done to people for centuries. Human nature. Nothing will ever change that."

I remembered her words because we'd had the argument over whether human nature was intrinsically good or evil many times. I believed that humans were born good, that the economic system we're born into, capitalism, with its emphasis on competition and profits over the needs of human beings and the environment, shaped our destructive impulses and led to wars over resources. My mother believed human nature was essentially evil. Reading her words anew, I found it easier to understanding why, after all the inhumanity and horror she'd witnessed, she believed as she did. I wondered if her philosophizing allowed her to distance her emotions from the memories of those bomb blasts, the fear that most surely had gripped her? If it was all just human nature, maybe she could believe she hadn't been scarred by the experience after all.

I shook the memory aside and kept reading.

"After that day, all of us, all the refugees from the camp, we all started going into the town. I think we took the ferry boat. Hundreds of Germans trying to get out of Berlin and other big cities were killed, the allies bombed hundreds. I saw them. That was a gruesome sight. That I remember. Arms and legs hanging all over the trees. Horses floating in big bomb craters."

My stomach lurched. My throat constricted. I could only read a paragraph or two, then I'd have to stop, try to remember to breathe.

"We heard stories that the Germans lost the war, that they were going to evacuate us, load up the ships in the harbor. Then the rumor started about Hitler committing suicide, and they let us board a ship. The Germans were loading the ships with all the food and machinery they could fit. The ship was taking all the German high officers, they were escaping, too. The officers and fourteen of us women. We were all spread out on deck, soldiers, the personnel, and all of a sudden the Allies started bombing. They hit three ships right close by us and the ships just split in half, folded, sinking and people were jumping overboard. People on other ships were trying to save them. I was just standing there, on the deck, watching. They were so close."

It could have been their ship, I thought, putting down the page, my hand shaking. They were so close to death. I would never have existed. They escaped and therefore I am. A precursor of me was on that ship. My mother, like every woman, was born with all her ova already present in her ovaries. The ovum that gave rise to me was present that day on the refugee ship, secreted away in the delicate recesses of my mother's body. I'd recently read an article about Epigenetics, research revealing how trauma is inherited through DNA, how stress hormones transform cells. Those bombs and exploding ships marked my genetic pattern, the trauma passed down to me. Just as Natalia's icy cold feet on the convent roof passed to my mother. A part of me had been on that convent roof, on that refugee ship. Did that explain my moods of despair, my depression? "Bull shit," my mother's voice, even though she was miles away in her own home, spoke loud and clear in my head. I knew she'd frown on my musings about inherited trauma, that she'd consider them a waste of time and self-indulgent. I ignored the familiar sting of rejection flushing hot on my cheeks and refocused on the transcript in front of me.

"The seas were very rough. We ate dried potatoes with water poured over them. Horrible food. Even so, I remember beautiful evenings. We sat on deck with a lot of young guys and there was a lot of singing. My mother was a nervous wreck because we were only fourteen women. But there wasn't anything going on. You just knew you were alive and you didn't even think that you might be dead the next day."

My spine tingled. I read that last sentence again. "You just knew you were alive and you didn't even think that you might be dead the next day."

What brilliant "being in the moment" my mother had been able to manage in the midst of such traumatic events, I thought. To take her attention off of the fear, to focus on the moment of being alive – wasn't that the essence of Zen, of the meditation practices I tried to incorporate into my own life?

During our unharmonious times together, I'd inwardly criticized her ability to ignore the elephant in the room, the way she'd buck up, refuse to confront the obvious problem in front of us. But there, on the ship deck, she'd honed the ability to focus only on the precise moment of life open to her. I'd seen it as a flaw, a way to skate out of conflict. I could see now that her tactic originated from a place of necessity, was a strength she relied on to survive under adversity. Why was I surprised she'd transferred that ability to the rest of life?

"We picked up sailors off life rafts, sailors from submarines who had survived torpedo attacks somehow." I continued reading. "Constantly bells rang to get ready to abandon ship, because the whole area was mined. One day we clambered down a rope to get on a transport ship, a barge, and they took us to another ship with many more refugees. Again, we were sitting in a huddle with our few possessions. Loudspeakers kept announcing this and that. My poor mother was beyond herself. She wasn't that old, about 50, but she couldn't handle things. She was very passive. I did everything. I had been the caretaker for quite a while."

No wonder my mother expected I'd never move away from her, I thought. My free spirit, moving around the US, putting my own needs ahead of hers, must have rubbed raw against the responsibilities she'd dealt with.

I turned back to the words on the page.

"I heard refugee camps were being organized, different camps for Poles, Latvians, Lithuanians, Estonians. Instead of being all together they split us up, because like any society, there are animosities. My mother wanted to go to the Polish refugee camp, thinking she'd find more lace-curtain Polish there. We found out how to get there, all by foot, there wasn't any transportation.

"My mother got a very rude awakening. The Poles who were able to run away from the labor camps, or who had been released, were just plain people, plain and loud and kind of rough. My mother saw this and she was very disappointed.

"Instead of staying there we went to a Latvian camp. Again, barracks, bunks, metal cabinets, the whole nine yards. But by that time the Americans and English were organizing the camps and there was food, clothing was delivered."

I picked up the embroidered cloth, ran my fingers over the raised red letters. I imagined my grandmother, a young Natalia, shivering on the convent roof, angry, sullen, pricking her finger with a needle, bringing it to her lips to suck the blood, plotting revenge on the world, indulging in her lace-curtain Polish fantasies. Instead of her dreams, she got a dead husband, three children to raise on her own, poverty, war and refugee camps.

Days later I framed the alphabet tapestry, red matting behind the white cloth to accentuate the ornate red letters, and hung it on my dining room wall, a reminder of dreams, hardships and reality.

The intricacy of the threaded letters, the loops and curves and knots, seemed to mirror the complexity of the lives of the two women, my grandmother and mother, who were so vital to my own existence. I vowed to renew my quest to learn more of their, and my, history.

Chapter 26

My mother's 84th birthday party at the Chateau La Jolla Inn was a festive affair. Her apartment, on the fourth floor with a big living room window facing toward the ocean, a few blocks away, brightened with sun rays and shimmering dust motes. My mother sat in a circle of friends, all women around her age, residents of the Chateau, as they called their home. My mother relished her move into a "Chateau" in her final years, at last achieving the royalty status she claimed her entitlement. She vowed she was the poorest resident there, her social security and pension barely covering the monthly rent, spending down the principle in her money market account. "I'm surrounded by millionaires," she'd say, proud of her comeuppance in the world from a penniless war refugee to a Chateau. At her birthday party she wore a paper tiara I nestled in her hair, crowning her queen for a day. I served up my signature carrot chocolate chip Bundt cake with cream cheese frosting. We all ate and drank champagne among my mother's most treasured possessions, trucked from Florida to San Diego – the coffee table Louie crafted from Greek and Italian tiles, a beaded lamp suited for a bordello, a 3-tier hanging basket of faux Tiffany glass we'd picked up in Taxco, Mexico, when I was thirteen, an inlaid wood music box. Candles burned in candlesticks from Yugoslavia and bouquets of flowers lent a floral fragrance to the air. Crystal candy dishes filled with roasted nuts sat atop a lace tablecloth from Florence, Italy. All artifacts of my mother's well-lived life.

What I remember most is how happy my mother was. She reigned over the gathering; her shock of white hair topped by the tiara, a necklace of large turquoise beads encircling her neck, her thousand- watt smile. Relishing the attention, she rose to the occasion with her quick wit, her ability to turn a phrase as she opened cards and small gifts from her new friends.

I liked her best when she was among her women friends, the focus off of me. One question from me could launch one of her friends into a cascade of stories from her life. An anecdote from one would trip off a tale in a similar vein from another. My mother was among her peers, the years they'd lived through, a shared history.

That was before arguments caused rifts between the women, before sides had been drawn, backs had stiffened. The honeymoon years at the Chateau. Before her friends had strokes, or worsening dementia, or had died. Before Lucy, my mother's treasured cat, passed.

*

"We didn't come through Ellis Island," my mother said. We were again walking together along the La Jolla coast.

I'd asked her to tell me more about her voyage from Germany to the US in 1949.

"We landed in Sharon, Connecticut. It wasn't a luxury cruise, that I can tell you. We were on a US Navy transport ship, very spartan. I was sea sick the whole time."

"And what was life like once you got to New York City?" I asked. She'd told me years before that she and her mother had been sponsored by a great aunt in New York and lived with her briefly.

"I don't want to talk about it," she replied. "I'm tired from all this talking. It brings up too many memories."

"Okay, Mom, I understand," I said, trying to catch her eye. She avoided my gaze, unclasped her hand from mine and searched through her purse for a tissue.

I was surprised by her answer. I'd thought we'd made it through the most difficult memories, the camps, bomb blasts and specter of death everywhere. She'd told me of life in Germany after the war, the food shortages, her job as a clerk in a porcelain factory. I'd thought life in New York would be a welcome relief, that she'd be happy to share her experiences. I'd heard, in small snippets of conversations over the previous decades, about her first job in New York at the Barricini Chocolate factory, a hilarious tale of working the assembly line. "I'd put one piece of chocolate in the box and one in my mouth," she'd laughed. "I arrived in New York skinny as a rail and after one month at Barricini's I couldn't button my skirt." I knew about her job as a model for Simplicity Patterns and her move up in pay when she landed a secretarial job at National Shirt Shops at their office in the Empire State Building in mid-town Manhattan. I'd heard vaguely about an apartment she and her mother shared next to the elevated subway line on the east side of Manhattan. But whenever I pushed for details, asked, "when did that happen, what year was that?" I'd get told, "Oh, I don't remember" or she'd shrug and turn away.

"Maybe another time," I'd reply, confused by her rebuff. "Let me know when you're ready."

But each time I'd asked in the months to come, she'd either changed the subject or professed she was too tired to talk. I'd thought it strange, but then again, I'd developed my own sixth sense for walking on egg shells around her moods, not pushing, not expecting too much.

Chapter 27

The women I was with scared the hell out of me. I was in Ajijic, Mexico, a quaint town full of Canadian and US ex-pats on Lake Chapala, near Guadalajara, for a writing workshop. A year and a half had passed since the initial shock of learning my paternal history. I was traveling with my writing mentor of thirty years, a widely-published author of several books and the leader of the writing workshop. The two of us were staying with her friend Judy, a well-known visual artist and author of a poetry blog, for a few days before the workshop began. Judy had offered to coach us in the art of retablo-making. I was in the company of two giants, creative and accomplished women. Their presence was a daunting challenge to my own fledgling creativity.

Believing in my creative ability had always been a stretch for me. Once, asked to draw a picture of my childhood self during an interpersonal psychology course I'd taken in my early twenties, I'd pictured myself sitting on a straight back chair, spine erect, eyes forward, hands folded in my lap, feet crossed at my ankles. Proper. Tamed. That was my mother's expectation of me – to be a good girl, not cause trouble. Now, knowing my birth history, I imagined she was very aware that Louie was taking me on – I wasn't his – and he had made clear the extra burden I presented. Perhaps if I melded into the background, Louie wouldn't notice I was there.

The creative spirt was wild. Untamed. I feared I couldn't let go of my conventional restraints and unleash my wild, creative side. I'd continued to pour my emotions into visual journals in the expressive arts group back home in San Diego; I knew the healing properties of art. But I wasn't where I hoped to be in my writing pursuits – no publications, still plugging away in classes and workshops.

Here, among my accomplished friends, I struggled to silence my inner critic. "You're an imposter," she snarked. "Just a wanna-be." Upon waking in the morning, alone in my bedroom, I voiced self-affirmations aloud. "I am worthy. My words matter," I'd counter her. I knew I needed to push myself past my comfort zone to overcome my fear.

"My Ajijic writer's group is hosting our monthly reading this Sunday," Judy mentioned to the two of us at our first dinner together. "Everyone gets to read fifteen minutes of original work. Newcomers welcome."

"I have a short story I'd like to read," I piped up. "Put me on the list."

A look passed between the two friends, their eyebrows raised.

"Why don't you give me your story tonight and I'll take a look," Judy said. She went on to extol the writing community in Ajijic, the quality of work read at past readings, who had just been published.

Feeling chastised, I fought the urge to demur and withdraw from the reader's list. A stubborn spark in me refused to back down. "Princess", my story about the death of a friend's horse, had been workshopped and edited over the last few years. Could "Princess" withstand Judy's scrutiny? Could I? Fear upped a notch in my throat.

The next morning we got started on our retablos. A retablo is a metal box surrounded by an embossed frame - an inner chamber and an outer frame. The outer dimension of mine was about the size of a piece of typing paper. The box, behind a hinged glass door, was an inch and a half deep. I knew what theme I wanted to explore in making my retablo – I wanted to make visual the journey I'd been on since finding out Louie wasn't my bio-father, to codify I was still me, regardless of the genetic forces acting on me. I was, after all, still the woman I'd become, still "me" – even though my inner DNA and chromosomes were different than I'd been told. Inner and outer. Put the inner, hidden, genetic self of myself in the inner compartment of the retablo behind the glass door. The part I had no control over. Three parental influences. I didn't have only one father. I had two. I could claim being both Italian and Jewish. I didn't want to parse which of the two had the most influence, just to make each one a viable presence. And on the outer frame, put expressions of myself that were the essence of who I was today.

"Where do I start?" I asked Judy.

"Just imagine your theme, and then find objects to bring it to life," Judy said.

Back in San Diego, I'd rummaged through old photos of my mother and Louie – what of them exemplified their personality, their core self? At the art table in Judy's living room, I took out the photos. My mother's studio portrait taken when she was twenty-six, her chubby nine-month-old illegitimate daughter, me, on her knee. Her toothy grin and satisfied smile belied any angst at being an unwed mother. For Louie, I'd chosen the photo of him sitting on the grass, legs stretched out in front, leaned back onto outstretched arms. The expression on his face captured what I remembered of him – aloof, staring off to the side. Not looking at the little girl, me at three, who sat at his side. For Ernie, the picture of him as a young sailor. I took scissors to the images, photocopied and shrunk them, added red to my mother's lips, brown to her hair. The work felt peaceful, and kindergarten came to mind; coloring, cutting and pasting. I hoped the motions would bring clarity and peace.

The three of us women were bent to our separate projects around a large dining room table covered in yellow plastic and strewn with tempera paint, brushes, stencils, pastels and glues. Mostly quiet, occasionally we'd share ideas and tips on what to do. Bird songs wafted in the large windows opening to magenta bougainvillea and a lush green landscape. The living room, like Judy's entire home, could well have been an art gallery. A wall painted the orange of a sunset displayed several of her retablos. Sculptures leaned in corners and African masks perched on ledges above the windows. The riot of colors and textures inspired my inner artist to come out and play.

In the tiny art studio behind Judy's house, shelf after shelf burst with Life and National Geographic magazines dating back decades, coins from foreign countries, maps from around the world. Old wooden library card-catalog cabinet drawers were stuffed with costume jewelry, puzzle pieces, tiny glass vials with tinier boats inside, ornate keys, miniature rubber animals, sailboats with miniscule lifejackets glued at the helm and more. A treasure-hunter's delight. What could I find to represent my three parents and myself?

I cut countries out of old maps – Latvia for my mother, Poland for Louie, Italy for Ernie – and shrunk them to paper the back of the metal box of the retablo with the origins of my ancestors. Months before, my new Italian cousin Carol had emphasized how much Ernie had loved his cocker spaniel. I found a small yellow rubber dog to glue near his photo. He had made his living, after leaving the merchant marines, putting up billboards. A tiny paint brush appeared. For Louie, a book, reminiscent of the Encyclopedia Britannica, and a sailing ship. For my mother, a tiny green wreath, like the wreaths worn atop the heads of summer solstice celebrants in Latvia, and beads of amber, of which she'd had many earrings and necklaces. Picking their trinkets wasn't hard. But who was I? What to put on the outer frame of the retablo? Who had I become in my 67 years of life? What made my heart sing? Besides being a mother, a companion to my husband?

I'd brought a photo of myself taken by my husband on a recent hike on the Saddlebag Lake loop trail in the high Eastern Sierra. In it, I stood in front of a glacier, hiking poles in my gloved hands, clad in a down jacket and woolen hat. A big smile on my face. At 10,000 feet in the Sierra, the hike had been challenging and the scenery jaw-dropping. I shrunk down the picture and, after securing it in a small gold frame, glued it to the outer metal frame of the retablo. Earlier I'd painted the frame in orange and yellows, taking a small brush to the raised details, the flowers and dots along the edges and corners, dabbing them blue and green.

I found a tiny United States passport to represent my love of travel to international destinations and a miniature book for my love of reading. Judy helped me shrink the actual pages of "Princess", my short story, and we secured them together with the tiniest paper clip imaginable. We fabricated a tiny writing pad and found an inch-long pencil. I'd brought two political buttons, from my activist days – "Money for Schools, Not for War" from the anti-Vietnam War movement and "Black Lives Matter" from the Showing Up for Racial Justice group I'd helped lead.

The finished retablo pleased me. It expressed, in three dimensions, my desire to integrate the pieces of my family saga. I could pick it up, run my fingertips over the edges, open the glass door to see my parents, close the door and see myself. Satisfied, I perched it on the night table next my bed and fell asleep.

*

The Ajijic writer's group met at La Nueva Posada on the hotel's restaurant patio under the branches of an enormous banyan tree. The tree's multiple thick trunks wound around each other and sprouted dozens of roots, which reached down to the ground like fingers, anchoring themselves to the earth. Its canopy of leaves spared us from the relentless burn of the sun. Woven baskets and strings of colorful lights hung from the banyan's boughs. Lilac flowers of blue sky vine cascaded over the hotel's white-washed brick fence, and beyond it, Lake Chapala graced us with a slight breeze.

We, the writers and audience, were all of a certain age, distinguished by our plumage - a jauntily angled wide-brimmed hat, a peacock feather, a sailor's cap. I wore an embroidered top purchased at the previous day's indigenous artist's faire. It seemed everyone knew each other and they chatted amiably as we took our seats around a few dozen tables. The aroma of freshly made tortillas and roasting chiles filled the air. My café de olla sloshed over the cup rim when I sat down, my leg bumping the rickety metal table atop uneven cobblestones. I was wired, and nervous.

In the evenings leading up to the reading, after we finished working on our retablos, I'd edited and re-edited "Princess". Judy, true to her word, had read my story and offered her critique. I'd worked hard to polish the piece and now, under the banyan tree, I was going to offer it up.

The mic screeched, and I heard a tap-tap-tap, signaling the reading was about to begin. I tried to focus on the readers before me, tried to quell my jitters, tried not to count down the list to my position - 7 - hopefully my lucky number. When my turn finally arrived, I was oddly calm. I read slowly. It wasn't until the last sentence that I choked, felt my face flush. I couldn't walk fast enough to reach the safety of my table. My friends both reached for my hands. It was then I noticed the applause.

Luckily, Judy wrote down comments made by people in the audience, because I couldn't absorb their words, let alone remember them. After the final reading, she read them aloud, looking right into my eyes. "Riveting, fascinating story and details. Felt like I was there the whole time." "Brave and courageous. Didn't let us look away." "Cinematic writing. I could see it all clearly. Powerful." Both our faces split wide open in smiles.

As the event was wrapping up, the editor of El Ojo del Lago, Ajijic's weekly magazine, asked me to send him "Princess" for publication. Others approached me to give their thoughts on the story. They'd taken my work seriously, commented on my use of metaphor and descriptions of the characters. I glowed inside.

Afterward, at lunch with five other writers, I felt like I belonged, had shown my mettle. I took a deep breath and let tears fill my eyes. The last eighteen months had been tumultuous and painful, my core identity shattered. I'd struggled to piece myself back to whole, one mosaic tile at a time. More and more, I could believe I was still "me" and that my "me" was truly okay.

Chapter 28

On my mother's eighty-fifth birthday, my sister and I took her to Los Angeles; a train ride, a fancy hotel near the Walt Disney Music Hall where the symphony played Tchaikovsky's Third Violin Concerto. We had dinner in a 1950s era Hollywood Italian restaurant with booths, the cracked red leather seats upholstered with large buttons. I cued the jazz combo to play "Happy Birthday" and a tuxedo-clad waiter presented a tiramisu aglow with candles. Always at her best as the center of attention, my mother glowed brighter than the candles.

My mother hosted me on a trip to Hawaii, a seven-day cruise around the islands. We gorged on the elaborate buffets, rented a car at ports to explore the beach towns. Trying to remain cheerful, I hid my exhaustion at our constant togetherness. My mother's incessant stream of chatter drained my patience. When I'd escape for an hour or two to take an on-board yoga class or to swim in the emerald green ocean, I'd return to her sour mood, piqued by my "abandonment".

At home in San Diego, many of our hours together were tinged with this same simmering tension about how I spent my time. In my early sixties, nearing retirement, I was still working full-time as a pediatric physical therapist. I struggled to balance my needs with my mother's expectation that we'd spend time together on weekends. That really wasn't so much, was it? Shouldn't I at least be able to see her once a week? On our phone calls during the work week, she'd take on a plaintiff tone if I didn't make a plan to see her. "What are you doing with your life that's so important?" she'd ask. I felt a constant pressure to please her. If two weeks would pass, she'd punish me when we did get together. "Oh, you decided to grace me with your presence?" she'd say, opening her door. Her foul mood would spill over to lunch at a café. She'd grouse about the service, snap at the waitress, complain about the food.

"We're all just waiting to die there," she'd complain about the Chateau, her independent living center. "What's there to do? I schlep to TJ Maxx to rummage through the racks. That's my only entertainment." I'd suggest an art class at a nearby museum, an excursion with others to the ballet. She'd glare at me and shake her head.

The little girl inside me, the girl who had born the weight of keeping her mother happy all those decades ago, still felt guilty for not performing up to snuff. No matter the years of therapy, no matter the rational explanations of logical boundaries; my instant, internal self-appraisal was "I'm not a good enough daughter". If only I paid more attention to her, if only I were more involved in her everyday life, if only I gave her more of my time, then she wouldn't be so sad. Why couldn't I just give her what she needed? Rearing up just behind the guilt, as reliable as moon rise after sunset, came white-hot anger and resentment.

I resented her expectations, resented that she imposed her needs so insistently in my life, resented her inability to make herself happy. At the same time, I battled with my resentment, knew it to be toxic to my own well-being. Why couldn't I open my heart wide enough to be her consistent companion? Maybe then she would finally relax, be content, be the kind, loving mother I longed for. Maybe her happiness was my responsibility after all. A tug-of-war raged within me and I was the rope.

Before driving to my mother's place on a weekend morning, I'd stand in front of my grandmother's hand embroidered alphabet tapestry, remember the war-torn, traumatic history in my mother's and her mother's past. I'd muster up empathy for my mother's high-strung nature. During the fifteen minute drive from my home to hers, I'd envisage my mother as a little girl sitting on the stoop of her home in Riga, anxious, twisting her braids. I'd conjure up compassion. Then, upon my arrival, she'd take one look at me and snark ,"Is that what you're wearing?" and the sharp edge of stone in my gut would rip open my resentment. My compassion out the window. Not that I'd speak my feelings aloud. That was still too risky, too forbidden. But my mother was a master at reading my face and body language, and our ensuing hours together would have a formal, tense edge.

Once, when she pouted at some perceived infraction of mine as I entered her apartment, I had the presence of mind to take her in my arms and hug her, wordlessly. She cried quietly on my shoulder for a few moments. Then she dried her eyes and smiled at me. "I'm reverting to a little kid," she said sheepishly. That small emotional release allowed us to have a good day together.

I thought that "reverting to a little kid", reinhabiting her life as a little girl and grieving for all she'd endured and lost, was exactly what my mother needed to do. The energy it took to suppress those feelings found an escape valve, like vapor, in her outbursts of self-righteousness, ire at the waiter in a café, the moue of her face when displeased at a blouse I was wearing. Wasn't that her own pain repressed and turned outward against others? Weren't we both two little hurt girls, each protecting our own territory, each too bruised to be able to give an inch to the other? In therapy, I gave my own inner child a voice, comforted her, tried to be my own loving parent so as not to expect my mother to fill that role. Why did I have to do all the work of changing?

I doubled my effort to encourage my mother to talk about the war, hoping she'd let loose, excavate the feelings underneath her edgy exterior. I hoped that were she able to speak aloud her dashed hopes of being a mathematician, the loss of her brother, the fear and horror at seeing death all around her, perhaps then she'd understand that her sadness stemmed from all that trauma.

"The past is the past," she squashed my inquires, as if she sussed out the motive behind them. "No use crying over spilled milk." She'd jump up, busy herself with the window blinds, change the subject. On my drive back home in the evening I mused about her response. Did she think if she felt the fear of those days on the ship deck watching the adjacent ships exploding that she'd never be able to pull herself out of the terror? That she'd be forever mired in sadness? Wasn't it selfish of me to bring up the past? Selfish of me to push her to recognize that her disappointments stemmed from her own history, not because I was a bad daughter? Selfish of me not to accept her as she was? Selfish of me not to rise above my own needs? Tug, tug, tug.

*

Four years after her move to La Jolla, my mother slipped in a grocery store and broke her lower leg. Three weeks after the fall, we were in her orthopedist's office, the first plaster cast removed, a second one being readied by the staff. I knelt before my mother, a bucket of warm water at my side, scrubbing the dead skin from her leg and foot.

"How fortunate you are to have your daughter nearby to help you," the doctor said when he entered the room.

"Well, I deserve it," my mother huffed, bristling. "I raised her you know."

The doctor shot me a look, eyes wide, eyebrows raised.

"You poor thing," I read in his look. Damn right, I silently agreed.

*

"The place I go to have my nails done closed down," my mother said one afternoon a few weeks after that doctor's appointment. We'd been thumbing through financial documents at her desk. She curled her wrists and fingers up towards her face, looking at her nails. "The arthritis, it's so bad, I can't do them myself anymore."

I did mental gymnastics in my head. A kind, loving daughter would find the manicure set, take her mother's hand in her own, massage her aching fingers, cut her nails. A kind, loving daughter would have a kind, loving mother, my resentment countered.

"There's a new nail salon behind the CVS drugstore," I said, ignoring the look on my mother's pain-stricken face.

Chapter 29

The framed 8 X 10 photograph of my biological father, Ernie Ferrino, occupied a prominent spot on a shelf above my writing desk. I'd often thought of the day my new Italian cousin Carol handed me the polka dot gift bag with the photo inside. I'd spent many hours of the two years since then examining Ernie's facial features, marveling at the likeness of the slant of our eyes and tilt of our smiles. Then I discovered Ernie wasn't my father after all.

Nick, my genealogist, had picked Ernie out of his family of five brothers because he had been the only sailor in the bunch. "I remember the guy was a sailor," my maternal cousin Ina told me those first days after discovering Louie wasn't my biological father.

"How can we be sure my father wasn't one of the other four brothers?" I'd asked Nick.

"We can't," he'd answered. "Not unless the children of those brothers would agree to be tested."

My skepticism proved prophetic. Nick had also said that, as the years progressed, new information might come to light. That was exactly what happened.

One day my email pinged with an alert from Ancestry.com about a new message for me on their internal message board. "My name is Callie. I am 35 years old. I believe we are connected through my biological father, Paul Ferrino, whom I've never met and isn't aware that I exist. I believe you might be my aunt. I was wondering if you could share some family history with me? I sincerely hope that you'll be in touch, it would mean so much to me."

My mind sped back to my first attempts to find my Italian relatives on Ancestry.com and the first query I posted on their message board. Callie's message struck the same plaintive tone I'd felt. I checked out the data on my Ancestry site and confirmed that our DNA connection was quite strong, much more so than that of my first cousins on my Italian side, just slightly less than my maternal half-sister Vicki. My curiosity piqued, I wrote her back with an invitation to call me anytime.

Callie called me the next day. After an awkward introduction, she said, "When I was thirteen, my mother told me that her husband, the guy I called Dad, was not my real father. She said my biological father was Paul Ferrino and he has never been a part of our lives. I never asked my mom much about Paul and then, when she got cancer and died soon after, it was too late." Callie words came in a rush, her emotion crackling over the many miles between us. "Now that my husband and I have three children, I want to know more about my real ancestry, so I sleuthed around and through distant relatives on 23andMe, found Paul. The fact that you and I are so closely related, DNA-wise, makes me think you and Paul may have the same father."

"Who was Paul's father?" I asked, expecting her to say Ernie Ferrino.

"Frank Ferrino," came her reply.

My stomach flipped over.

"Does Paul know that for sure?" I asked.

"Frank signed Paul's birth certificate but did not have any part in raising him. Paul never met him. But Paul's mother often talked about him."

The importance of Callie's news began to sink in. If Frank Ferrino was Paul's father, and Paul was my biological half-brother, that meant Frank, not Ernie, was my father, too.

I opened the family tree book my cousin Carol gave me all those months ago when we'd first met. Frank, Ernie's younger brother, was the fifth son born to my grandparents. I had met Frank's two daughters on a zoom call several months before. At the time, we thought we were first cousins. If Frank, not Ernie, was really my biological father, those "cousins" were really my half-sisters! And Paul Ferrino was my half-brother.

"Paul sent in his DNA sample to Ancestry.com last week," Callie said. "He had no idea I even existed, doesn't even remember my mother, apologizes to me constantly. When his DNA results come back we'll know for sure whether he's really my father. And whether you and he are really half-siblings, too."

I barely heard her words. "Frank" echoed in and out of my head.

I stared at Ernie's photo long after Callie and I said goodbye. Not my father? What about that jolt of recognition, the surge of kinship I felt when Carol handed me his photo all those months ago? Were my feelings just the emotional overflow of a brain wanting to believe, wanting to belong? Had they been manufactured, manipulated by adherence to a story pulled out of the hat by a genealogist wanting to wrap up an assignment? Embarrassment and shame flooded through me. I burst into tears. I had duped myself. Duped myself into accepting a biological connection to a man based on a false premise, on a surge up my spine. I'd made the mistake of acting on emotion rather than logic. Had I? I wouldn't know for sure until Paul's DNA results came in. And if I could dupe myself into believing I was connected to the wrong father, what difference did it make if I found out who the "real" father was?

Chapter 30

My mother and I sat across the table from each other, another restaurant lunch together, a frequent weekend excursion since she had moved from Florida to an independent living center near my home in San Diego. This time it was an Italian place. My mother picked around the lasagna on the plate in front of her.

"Why am I still alive?" she asked me. "What for?" Deep furrows pulled down the corners of her lips. Her hazel eyes, usually alert and bright, were dull and flat.

My mother's best friend at the center had recently died, leaving her without a ready companion to share a glass of wine before dinner, without a buddy with whom to dig through racks at the local thrift stores. Still physically spry for her age, she lamented that she no longer had the pep she once felt. She'd lost interest in even the activities that used to bring her the most joy. She declined my invitation to the symphony earlier in the month, said she didn't feel up to a weekend trip to Los Angeles, poo-pooed the idea of joining a chair exercise group at her living center.

"Been there, done that," she'd said.

When I'd probed deeper, asked her to consider that she might be depressed, she'd glared at me, then given me her usual opinion on the subject of psychological analysis.

"Bullshit. The doctor asked me if I wanted an antidepressant. Is a pill going to make me young again? I'm not depressed. I'm old."

It wasn't the first time she'd said she was fed up with life.

"Lucky Sylvia," she'd said the week before, referring to her friend at the center who'd died. "She had a heart attack in her sleep, went fast. That's how I want to go, the sooner the better."

"I'm sorry you're so unhappy, Mom," I looked her in the eye across the dining room table, tried to say something neutral, but supportive.

"It's like I'm an inmate in jail. This old-age home is like death row. I'm just waiting for my turn to die. I'm lonely and bored. What's the point?"

That morning, I'd called to let my mother know I'd be a half-hour late to pick her up. She'd greeted me at her door with a clenched jaw and icy stare.

"I'm starving," she said, petulantly. "I had no idea you'd be so late."

"Did you have breakfast?"

"A little left-over croissant. Now the day is half over." She held her body rigid.

Her message was clear. I wasn't doing enough for her. I'd doused the flare of anger in my gut, not wanting to start the afternoon with a tiff.

But now, as I sat across the crisp, white linen tablecloth from my mother, my emotions somersaulted. I took in her grief-laden face, the defeat in her eyes. Aging is a bitch, I thought. I wanted to help but had no idea how. I still smarted from her ill-tempered greeting an hour before. My eyes filled with tears for both of us. I moved the garlic bread out of the way, reached across the table, and took her hand in mine, the skin between her fingers whisper soft, like wrinkled crepe paper. I didn't dare open my mouth, didn't trust what words might come out. A loving gesture was all I could manage.

"I wish I lived in Oregon," she said, her voice a croak. When I'd arrived at her apartment that morning, the TV blared with a CNN news report about the legalization of assisted suicide in Oregon.

"Are you saying you're considering suicide?" I asked, trying to keep my voice level.

"Argh, don't use that word," she admonished, pulling her hand from mine as if I'd scalded her.

*

Only a couple of months after that lunch at the Italian restaurant where my mother questioned her reason for living, she lay in a hospital room, her lungs filling up with liquid, having refused intubation or antibiotics to address her pneumonia. All she wanted was pain medication.

I had spent the previous four days at her bedside at her apartment, doling out cough medicine, taking her temperature, helping her into adult diapers once she felt too weak to make it to the bathroom at night on her own. I fed her chicken soup.

"Oh, it's horrible," she'd complained. "The chicken is like shoe leather. No flavor."

I'd put only the tiny noodles, vegetables and broth on the spoon, cupped my hand underneath to catch the drips. Her mouth quivered, opened in anticipation of my spoon. Her short, white hair stood up at odd angles against the pillow.

"See how things have changed," she'd said, her feverish fingers cuffing my wrist. "I used to feed you."

We waited a couple of days before going to the emergency room. She didn't want to go and I didn't push it, even though I thought she was getting worse rather than better.

During those few days, I'd remembered her reference to Oregon, to euthanasia, wondered if maybe this was her own private Oregon. I felt an unspoken collusion between us. I felt it when I said, "Mom, you seem a little worse today. Maybe it's time we go to the ER." And she said, "No, not yet," and set her jaw. Was she waiting until she knew she'd be too sick to recover without an invasive procedure? She had Do Not Resuscitate orders on file at the hospital and didn't want any heroic measures taken to save her life. I felt our collusion when she said, "This cough is wearing me out. Give me more cough medicine", cutting her eyes at me only for a second, daring me to say no. And even though it'd been only an hour since her last dose, I'd given her another heaping spoonful. I didn't voice my conjecture. I worried I was misreading her intentions. Still, the energy around us crackled with a charged frequency, as if we each knew what she was planning, but didn't risk saying it out loud. I'd remembered her admonition when I'd used the word "suicide" months before. In my own mind, I battled out the ethics of what I was doing. Was I hastening her death? Killing her? Should I insist on getting medical help? How could I live with myself if I didn't do everything possible to save her? But this is what she wants, I'd counter with my own argument. She is tired of living. She knows this is her way out. Wasn't it better to get it over with?

"The doctor said it was just the flu," she'd said, when I questioned her about an appointment she'd had with her geriatric physician earlier that week.

"Not so," the same doctor told me days later outside her hospital room when it was clear hospice arrangements needed to be made.

"I told her I thought she had pneumonia and needed a chest x-ray," he said. "I wanted her to take an antibiotic. She'd laughed and said it was just a cold." His words assuaged my guilt at having waited to call the ambulance.

Instead of going to the hospital, for a few days we'd cuddled in bed together, watching Jimmy Stewart and Cary Grant in old movies on Turner Classic Movies. I rearranged her pillows, opened and closed the window blinds to keep the sun out of her eyes, changed her sweaty nightgown for a fresh one, urged her to sip water from a straw, fed her. She often reached for my hand, said she loved me. Finally, one morning she told me she was having trouble taking a breath.

"That's it," I said, not giving her a chance to argue. "I'm calling an ambulance."

Lying on a gurney in the ER, my mother whispered to me "You are a wonderful woman and a wonderful daughter and you've done everything you could for me." Our hands were clasped, our heads close together. I started to cry. I'd been waiting my entire life to hear those words from her.

When she was transferred to a private hospital room, started on morphine, I set up a CD player, and put on the Schubert symphonies she loved. I lay next to her on the bed, retelling stories about our cruises to Alaska and Hawaii, how we'd gorged ourselves at the midnight chocolate buffet. I massaged her hands and arms with Aveeno, the skin on her forearms ridged, creased and lined like layers of sandstone in a desert.

"I love you so much," she said. "How did you get to be so wonderful? How did you do it? You are my guardian angel. An atheistic miracle."

Incredulous at her pronouncements of love and her recognition of my basic good nature, I reveled in her words. Finally, I had the mother I'd always wanted. At the same time, I was heartbroken that my mother was on her deathbed and that time for our relationship to deepen had run out. Why couldn't we have had this closeness the last few years? If only I'd been able to overcome my defensiveness and open my heart without reservation. Would she have felt that and softened to me earlier?

I swabbed her dry, caked lips with moistened pink foam on a stick. Her bird-beak mouth puckered around the swab.

"Dip that in champagne," she said, still managing an impish smile. Her trembling hands, hot, reached for mine.

My husband and brother-in-law, recently arrived from New York, brought a bottle of champagne, and our small family and two good friends, standing at the foot of her bed, made toasts with plastic glasses as my mother slurped her last bubbly off a pink swab.

"What happened?" She sat straight up in bed after everyone but me had left. "I want to get out of here." I put my hand on her chest, felt the gurgling of liquid as she inhaled a breath and called a nurse to administer more morphine.

I took out her dentures. "Where are your teeth?" she asked me, eyes wide open in alarm. I brushed the hair off her widow's peak, murmured words of comfort in her ear.

"I had the most exquisite day," she whispered as I prepared to go home and get some rest. She lay against the pillow, lower jaw sunken, mouth open, her lips purple and thin. I could see the exposed ridged roof of her upper palate. My mother had hidden her vulnerability all my life. Now she was so fragile, so enfeebled. The change was so stark, hard to fathom.

My sister Vicki arrived from New York the next day. By then, my mother hardly spoke, the morphine needed to prevent panic as her lungs filled with fluid was keeping her sedated. Vicki never got the bedside laudatory words of love and appreciation my mother bestowed upon me. Most of the day was spent figuring out next steps: a nursing home or home care? The hospital needed her bed and was discharging her soon.

The next morning, I awoke with the certainty I had to get straight with her, say the truthful words about her terminal condition.

I sat in a chair pulled up close to her bed, held her hands.

"We have to say goodbye," I said to her. "You are dying. You are in hospice. I love you. I know you are ready to go. It is time."

Up until then, after the ER and the "comfort care only" measures had been implemented by doctors respecting my mother's wishes that no invasive, life-saving procedures be used, I had not said the actual words: Dying. Goodbye. Time to go.

I had said only "sick, pneumonia and try to rest."

Our eyes locked, hers from sockets that seemed to excavate her skull. Tears streamed down my face. She squeezed my fingers. Little downy, white hairs on her chest caught the light streaming from the window. Her sunken collar bones made canyons of her neck.

On her last day in the hospital, my mother struggled to breathe. I helped her sit up in bed, my elbow crooked behind her back, her head so tiny it fit in the palm of my hand, grey and white short hairs spiking up.

"Who's flying the plane?" she asked, her words, the first uttered in over 24-hours, clear as a bell.

"I think you are," my sister, standing at her bedside, said.

My mother was quiet.

"You're flying the plane, mom," I said. "Where are you going?"

"To a better place," she answered.

"Stop the world, I want to get off," she'd often said when we'd watched the news on TV together at my home or hers. "Too much horror."

She's exiting the world on her own terms, I thought, floored by her steel will, her will to make a conscious decision to choose death over life.

That evening, an ambulance brought my mother back to her apartment, where I'd arranged for hospice care to begin.

"I don't expect her to live for more than a few days," her doctor had said during the hospital discharge.

I left my mother in the care of a hospice RN, the word "compassion" tattooed on her inner wrist. Where was my compassion? I berated myself as I drove home late that evening. I was leaving my dying mother in the care of strangers.

In the middle of the night, I sat up in bed with a start, checked the time. Three a.m. Go, I thought. Go to her apartment right now. What if she's dying right now? I didn't listen to my inner voice. Instead, I tried to go back to sleep. Forty-five minutes later I stopped fighting my impulse, dressed in the dark room, not wanting to wake my husband, and got in the car. I was half-way to her apartment when I got the call. "Your mother just passed away."

Devastated I'd missed her final breath, I sobbed in the arms of the nurse, my mother's body still warm in the bed at our side, a sheet pulled up to just under her chin, all her skull's hollows – cheekbone and temple and jaw – shadowed in grey.

The transport guy from the cremation company came at noon with a collapsed gurney, wearing a somber three-piece suit, greased back hair. Without ceremony, he wrapped my mother in a sheet, mummy-like, head-to-toe, then billowed a second sheet over her and tucked in the edges. He strapped seat belt-like straps across her chest, hips and ankles, rolled her out of her apartment, feet first, down to the elevator.

"You'll never get me to go to a nursing home," she'd said several times in the last year. "The only way I'm ever moving out of my apartment is feet first." She'd gotten her wish.

The large elevator in the building was out-of-order, so we had to make do with the small one. A 5x5 foot elevator. A six-foot gurney. The guy stood in front of the open door, sweat glistening on his temples. He raised the gurney to almost vertical; it lurched forward. My mother's body strained against the straps. He rushed to stand in front of her, to stop the toppling, and then pushed and shoved and jammed my mother into the corner of that elevator, at an odd angle. He spread his arms to keep her in place, panting.

"Please push the button," he said, head down, not meeting my eyes.

I did, then ran down the stairs to see him roll her into a non-descript white van and pull away. And so, my mother left me.

*

My first shower since my mother's death, I thought to myself the day after my mother died. I leaned against the walls of the shower stall to steady my body racked with sobs, washed off the smell of her, her musk and illness and dying. She's gone, she's gone. My first walk at the beach since my mother's death. She's gone, she's gone. Where did she go?

She still inhabited my mind. How did cars still jam the freeways, how did people crowd stores, buy groceries? It felt disloyal to talk to anyone, to smile or laugh knowing that she was dead. How could the world just go on in the absence of her big presence?

I thought of resentments – those my mother had of me and my sister Vicki and how we didn't pay enough attention to her. Resentments born of the lack of attention, the trauma she suffered as a child. After listening to a meditation CD on forgiveness, I was faced with my own resentment – my resentment of my mother for expecting so much of me, for needing me so much, for imposing herself so insistently in my life. And yet I knew how hard it was to love without expectations. How could I have expected her to love me without her enormous needs? That was who she was, the Ludy-ness of her.

I'd carried a hardness in my heart, when I'd been around her. I had to begin the work of forgiving her and, even more difficult, forgiving myself. Why hadn't I evoked more childhood stories from her, let her ramble on? If only I hadn't taken personally, as if it were my fault, her misery at aging, the affront to her dignity.

Jim, the driver at the Chateau La Jolla Inn, once told me, "When I'd pick your mother up at the doctor's she'd say 'don't take me back to the Chateau. It's like jail. Let's go someplace else'". He didn't take that personally. I did, when she'd said the same thing to me. I took her words as a black stain against my character, my lack of time and attention to her. I resented her resentment. Even though, those last years of her life, I'd worked on opening my heart,

I never could sustain acceptance, unconditional love of her. I'd needed more time. I was getting closer, but I hadn't yet arrived. Forgiving her? Forgiving myself was much harder.

*

I learned of my paternal parentage four years after my mother's death. Once my initial anger at her lies and betrayal ebbed, the knowledge re-opened my box of regrets about my feelings and actions during the last few years of her life. I had spent hours in therapy examining her narcissism and recognizing its toxic effect on our relationship. Yet, I now wondered, had I been able to show her unconditional love, might she have softened and told me about my biological father? When she'd been angry when I arrived late to pick her up for lunch, if only I'd remembered her anger came from a place of hurt and fear. If only I'd held her in my arms. If only the seeds of resentment inside me hadn't tightened me up, pissed me off, clouded my thinking.

I relived the last few days of my mother's life and again, reveled in her open declarations of love for me. She appeared in my mind's eye as a twenty-five-year-old, war-scarred immigrant in a new country, lying in a home for unwed mothers. She held her newborn baby girl, swaddled, in her arms, stroked the fuzz on my cheeks. My unfocused eyes sought hers.

"She's mine. I'll keep her," she insisted to the nuns advising adoption. Her heart cracked open with love as my tiny fingers encircled her thumb. She adored me, could not imagine letting me go. She would do anything necessary, face the fire a 1950s America had for unwed mothers and illegitimate children, to keep me. The will power she needed to survive her war-torn country, to survive displaced person camps and refugee ships, that steel will bolstered her decision.

On her deathbed, she openly adored me. "My atheistic miracle," she'd said. And I gave her all of myself, cared for her with devotion.

At the portals of life and death, our most profound transformations, my mother and I were open and the truth ensued – our want, our need, our love – revealed. The remainder of time, life between the two portals, our receptivity slammed shut, the risk of exposure too great. Steel will stiffened her spine. She guarded her secret, masked her vulnerability. I reacted, rigid as well.

But at the gossamer edges, the edge of birth, the edge of death, our love flowed freely, osmosed like ether through our entire selves. We gave to each other the essence of our being, the great gift of pure love.

Chapter 31

Three and half years had passed since finding out Louie wasn't my biological father. For two years Ernie Ferrino filled those shoes. Now, DNA evidence indicated that Ernie's brother Frank had most likely been my father. The morning after my new niece Callie divulged the revelation about Frank, I opened the local newspaper to find a splashy front- page article: "Condors reproduced without mate: For first time, scientists learn birds can have offspring asexually." I burst out laughing. My mother may as well have had me asexually, for all the good father-figures have been in my life, I thought. I read the article aloud to my husband Walter at our breakfast table.

"A scientific team led by the San Diego Zoo Wildlife Alliance announced Thursday that California condors can reproduce without having sex. Researchers made the finding after genetic tests showed that two condors born in captivity didn't have fathers.

"Yes, fathers. And that's not a misspelling of feathers.

"This phenomenon, known as parthenogenesis, has been seen in certain insects, fish and reptiles. There have been a few cases among birds, too. But no one knew until now that female California condors could have offspring without males, a head-scratching finding that raises questions around how often this occurs and whether it matters in the wild.'"

"The real question," I snarked to Walter as, suddenly full of energy, I jumped up and paced our hallway, "is whether the origin of the sperm matters one hoot in any case!"

*

Intrigued by the quirky idea of a female reproducing without a male, I spent the weeks waiting for Paul's DNA results researching parthenogenesis, the word itself derived from the Greek words for "virgin birth". Several ancient Greek and Roman myths revolve around female deities who spawn progeny without males. Hesiod, a Greek poet, who lived around 700 BC, around the same time as Homer, wrote epics considered a major source of Greek mythology. Four of Hesiod's female deities reproduced parthenogenetically.

My favorite myth was that of the Hindu goddess Durga, the goddess of female empowerment. Unable to slay the many demons haunting her domain, needing an ally, she birthed her daughter Kali out of her forehead.

I wished my mother had seen me as an ally, as a slayer of the false prophets that put us in the box of "unwed", "bastard", and "illegitimate". If only she had trusted me with her truth so we could have, together, at least made an attempt to throw off the aspersions we faced. If only we'd had that bond of camaraderie.

It made sense, given the fact that babies emerge from their mother's bodies, that early creation myths would assume the primacy of the female. The fact that reproduction is initiated by the fusion of a male's sperm and female's ovum wasn't fully understood until the late 1800s. When did the role of the biological father assume importance? I knew that human society began as matriarchal, with women raising children communally without a central father figure. When in human history did the relationship between the father and child become sacrosanct? Did my longing to find my biological father spring from a natural, primal need? Or were my feelings an ideological construct of the patriarchal culture in which I was raised?

At what point in history did having a "daddy" tug at a child's sense of self-worth? When did the word "bastard" arise? When did "illegitimate" and "unwed mother" take their place in the vernacular?

Why did I pine for a Daddy?

Chapter 32

When I was in my mid-twenties, in 1973, I joined the Young Socialist Alliance, a nation-wide group dedicated to building a movement of young workers and students to bring about the transformation from capitalism to socialism. I lived with three other women, all of us political activists, in the Mission District of San Francisco, a neighborhood with activists of many stripes. It was a heady time. The second wave of the women's movement was in full swing and women friends and comrades were the central focus of my life. Although the Supreme Court ruling on Roe v Wade had just legalized our right to abortion, the Equal Rights Amendment had yet to be ratified. We organized a Day in the Park for Women's Rights in Golden Gate Park and I spoke in front of thousands of supporters to demand passage of the ERA. We marched in the largest ever Gay Pride Parade in San Francisco. The struggles to end apartheid in South Africa and to win union representation for farmworkers in California were big issues at the time, and we traveled across the state to lend a hand.

The intensity we gave to our political work was matched by the fun we had together - women's softball games and bar-b-ques in the Oakland hills, dancing and playing pool at Peg's Place in the Outer Sunset, late night runs to the corner store for popcorn to fuel our penchant for *Mary Hartman, Mary Hartman*, a sit-com that left us in stitches – it seemed there was always a party happening somewhere. My life was full and I felt powerful and happy.

Now, decades later, my mind swirling with questions about how my search for a Daddy might be linked to the patriarchal culture I was born into, I remembered those years of activism and the revolutionary ideas I'd soaked up. I dug around in the garage to excavate a box of old political books, excited to find Woman's Evolution: From Matriarchal Clan to Patriarchal Family by socialist, feminist and scholar Evelyn Reed. I dusted off the cover and began what turned out to be a valuable reference in my search for answers to my many questions about fatherhood.

Published in 1975 during the second wave of feminist activism, Reed was a forerunner of feminist scholars writing on women's issues of her day. At the time, the existence or non-existence of matriarchy was a hotly contested issue in anthropology. Reed reinvestigated volumes of existing anthropological research to come to the conclusion that the maternal clan system was indeed the original form of social organization and that during this time women held a highly esteemed and influential place. Her research traced how women lost their social eminence and became the subordinate sex as our ancestors made the transition to patriarchal society.

The first eye-opener was Reed's detailed research on the evolution of the role of men as fathers and husbands. Our early ancestors were unaware of biological paternity. Fatherhood as a social institution did not begin on the basis of sexual intercourse between a man and woman. To the primitive mind children were not the fruit of a momentary act of sexual congress but of years of patient nurture and care.

Sex had little to do with marriage in the formative stage of its development. Sex play among youths was seen as natural and was unrestricted in the community. Before a man could be promoted from the status of sex partner to husband he had to be accepted by the mother of his female partner. A marriage began when a pair ate food together. Food intercourse was the mark of a pair-bond.

The word "matrimony" means mother-marriage. Women initiated marriage. If a woman's mother approved, her mate moved into her community.

The origin of the word "husband" is gardener or farmer, tasks the man was given to help his wife's community thrive. Marriage developed side by side with farming and animal husbandry. Once a male became the husband of the mother, he was advanced to the status of "male mother". His social functions were to help feed, nurture and protect his wife's children.

Reed concluded that, "Paternity began as a social relationship between a woman's husband and her child" (472). "Thus fatherhood as a social institution did not begin on the basis of sexual intercourse between a man and a woman but as a set of maternal functions performed by the man for his wife's child" (475).

The sentences leapt off the page, exploded in my mind and lit fireworks down my spine. If there was no "social relationship", there was no "fatherhood". Here it was, the answer to my question "What difference did finding out about Ernie, or now possibly Frank, make?" He had no social relationship with me, therefore he wasn't my father! The alignment of cells deep in my bone marrow shifted. If there was no "social relationship", there was no "fatherhood," I repeated out loud over and over. The sentence felt heretical. Disloyal to fathers. In my concept of father, biology was a key factor.

My son Eli had known about his conception by sperm donor for over fifteen years. I'd asked him several times if he wanted to find his biological father and his emphatic answer was always, "No. I already have a father. Walter is my dad. That other guy is just not in the picture."

"Walter is Eli's only father," my mother had chided me when I told her Walter and I told Eli about his birth history.

Was my mother right after all?

How did the word "father" become attached to the biological act of procreation? Why did children of my generation watching the sit-coms of the 1950s and 1960s assume that Ward, Beaver's father on *Leave It to Beaver* was Beaver's biological father? Why was I so driven to find my "true" father?

The questions in my head wouldn't leave me alone. I kept returning to Reed's research, pulled to understand human history. Was this the way to make sense of my own personal journey? Could I balance this intellectual pursuit without getting too much "in my head" and ignoring my heart? Perhaps if I could lay my own mother's decisions to shield herself and me from the truth of my paternity in the bosoms of the mothers and daughters that came before us, maybe then I could make a lasting peace with my mother and finally rest.

Why, I wondered, when women were at the height of their power and prestige, did power come into the hands of the men and not the women? How did men establish their supremacy in society and the family? How did the stigma of "unwed" mother and "bastard" child arise from our female-centered history? Why would my mother have felt compelled to re-invent my paternal history?

Reed theorizes that the basis of women's downfall lies in the rise of the concept of private property, which paralleled the evolution from matriarchy to patriarchy. As our species evolved from nomadic, hunter-gatherers to farmers and animal herders, we began to amass wealth from our agriculture and animals. The concept of "ownership" arose and was extended to land and property. Along with ownership came power and control.

A key factor preventing women from maintaining control of property and power was the development of the marriage gift into purchase marriage. Marriage gifts were originally the primitive interchanges of food and other items to bring hostile groups of men together, a necessary precondition for matrimonial relations. At a certain point this gift-giving passed over into a new and different kind of transaction – the exchange of what had become personal property. The marriage gift became the bride price. The terms "bride price" and "purchase marriage" refer to the practice of exchanging property for a woman in marriage.

Bride price was the first factor behind the rise of private property in male, not female hands. Whereas a woman previously made the decision about the man she married, with the advent of purchase marriage the woman's wishes were of little or no account. Men made the deals and marriage contracts.

Patriarchal class society was founded upon the family, private property, and the state. Property brought wealth and both property and wealth exerted control over others. Family inheritance of that property and wealth ensured continuation of control. The two went hand in hand. Eventually, nation states consolidated and legalized both private property and the father-family with its line of descent, inheritance and succession from fathers to sons. Monotheistic religions, with their emphasis on the one father family gained prominence to further legitimize the system.

The bride price later changed to include payment for the children of the bride, useful for providing labor and future laborers. All this was happening before facts about biological paternity became known. A man "begot" a child not through a genetic process but through a property transaction.

The wife who wanted to leave her husband found it increasingly difficult to do so because children were involved.

Sexual jealousy – not prevalent in matriarchal society – developed side by side with private property and the patriarchal family. The husband now owned his wife and had exclusive rights to her sexual organs as well as her children; they were part and parcel of his property. With the full development of private property and the patriarchal family, women lost control over their lives, their destinies and even their own bodies.

The downfall of women brought about a sharp reversal in their value as wives. In place of the bride price, the payment made by a husband to secure a wife, families offered a dowry as an inducement for men to marry their daughters. Now the dependent wife paid the price to secure a husband and provider.

The scope and enormity of what I was learning demanded my complete attention. I read and re-read passages of <u>Women's Evolution</u>, outlining in detail what I gleaned, trying to fathom the complexity of the information. I sought out other sources on anthropology and human evolution. In order to digest the glut of facts and theory, I had to keep reminding myself that changes happened over eons of time, that the various strands of history – the change from a matriarchal to patriarchal line, the development of farms and animal husbandry, the amassing of personal property and wealth, the onset of bride price – all these changes were braided together over millenniums at different paces in different parts of the globe. The phrase "the personal is political", which I'd adopted early in my days of feminist consciousness raising, kept repeating in my head. I was convinced I was on the right track in making sense of my own personal journey to recover a sense of my identity since the revelations about my father.

*

The evolution to patriarchy is still going on in our present era. Until China's Cultural Revolution of the 1960s and 1970s, the Mosuo, a Chinese ethnic minority of about 40,000 people high up in the Himalayas, lived for hundreds of years with a complex social structure that valued female power and decision-making. The head of a Mosuo household was always a woman, responsible for all financial decisions and the passing of the family name and property. Among Mosuo traditions is the practice of the "walking marriage". Women may choose and change partners as they wish. Mosuo children stay with their mothers' families for life and men only visit their female partners by walking to their houses at night. The Cultural Revolution banned the Mosuo religion and forced couples to marry. Today the Mosuo straddle the change from their matriarchal society to the new reality. Women hold no official political power. Fewer women are able to sustain a way of life traditionally centered on large, matrilineal clans sharing their household income.

Will the coming generations of Mosuo children be forced to deal with the stigma of "bastard" and "illegitimate" as the winds of change blow through their culture? Will their mothers be squeezed into making hard choices to protect the well-being of families?

In Western culture, especially in the white, Anglo-Saxon Protestant dominant culture of the United States in which I grew up, focus on patriarchy and the nuclear family soared as the engines of big business needed each family unit to purchase separate washing machines, dryers, lawnmowers and cars to grease their profit machines. The media did its job to cement the idealized concepts of the nuclear family into the zeitgeist. *Leave It to Beaver*, *Father Knows Best* and *The Brady Bunch*, popular television sit-coms of the 1950s, 60s and 70s, played in living rooms throughout the US, all portraying kind, if slightly befuddled, dads, well-meaning, good providers with always a caring ear for their offspring's woes. Who wouldn't pine for a daddy like that? No wonder I'd been driven to find him.

*

The sting of my own personal situation lessened as I put myself in the context of human history. My longing to know my "true" father was tethered to the social and economic system in which I was raised. My brain synapses had been primed by those forces to create emotions that reflected the material world around me. It wasn't illogical for me to want to find my biological father. But the urgency I'd felt to do so fizzled in light of all I'd learned.

I had come to understand that my mother's anxiety and personality traits were in large part a product of war and its underpinning, the greed for resources under our profit-driven economic system. Her individual story, broadened out into the wider context of what was going on in the world around her, radiated outward in concentric circles: the death of her father, the resultant poverty of her family, WWII, displaced persons camps, bombs, immigration to a new country, an out-of-wedlock pregnancy. Not that all in her life was traumatic. She did, after all, end up a middle class, well-traveled woman living in a "Chateau". But the traumas she endured infused our relationship, fueled the discord and dissonance, the secrets and lies. My focus on the societal forces acting on my mother led me to question the impact of the societal forces acting on me. I discovered that, in large part, the emotions driving my search for my "true" father were a product of those same forces, namely patriarchy and capitalism.

My mother did what she could to provide me with a father. She, a product of her moment in history, protected me from the sting of "bastard" and herself from "unwed mother". Her early upbringing under Stalinism and war, fighting for survival in displaced persons camps of post-war Germany, was a time rife with deception and the cover of lies. Had she lived to experience the ease with which one can pinpoint paternal heritage, perhaps she would have told me the truth of my paternity. Instead, in her moment in history, her lies gave her, and me, as a child at least, shelter.

My moment of history allowed me to expose her lies. I came of age in the United States in the 1960s – the second wave of the feminist movement, women's consciousness raising groups, social liberation and civil rights struggles, all with an emphasis on openness and freedom.

My mother and I were on two different shifting tectonic plates of human history, swayed and buffeted by conflicting forces. My heart rests on the conviction that we did the best we could to hang on to each other as we weathered the gale force winds of change.

Chapter 33

On my seventieth birthday I got the news from Ancestry.com that Paul Ferrino was indeed my half-brother. He and I shared 2,164 centimorgan and 31% of our DNA, even more than my maternal half-sister Vicki and I shared. Just to be sure, I sent Nick, my former genealogist, an email with the results. No doubt about it, he replied. I now had conclusive proof. Frank Ferrino, not Ernie, was my biological father.

The news didn't have the sting I had felt a few weeks before when Callie raised the possibility. My dive into the evolution from matriarchy to patriarchy had taken me out of myself, out of my own confusion and pain, and given me a more global perspective, reinforced my belief that the personal is political.

"Oh well," I said to Ernie's photo, still smiling at me from my book shelf. "Who knows what I'll discover next."

Texts flew between Paul, Callie and me as we arranged a zoom meeting for the following evening. I was going to meet my brother! And even more momentous, Callie was going to meet her father.

"Unreal," Paul and Callie said simultaneously when our images appeared on the screen. They both had tears in their eyes. Paul looked just like the photo he had sent me earlier. Handsome, with salt and pepper curly hair cut short above a high forehead, he had a matching mustache below a fleshy nose, a white close-cut beard and wide cheekbones. I wasn't struck by any resemblance between us. Brianna, Paul's other daughter, was also on the zoom call. The resemblance between her and her half-sister Callie was striking, both of them beautiful, with high cheekbones, big brown eyes and dark hair. In addition to a new half-brother, I also had two new half-nieces.

"I was born in Mt. Vernon, New York in August of 1950," Paul answered my first question.

"Six months before I was conceived," I said after doing the calculation quickly in my head. "Looks like Frank was a busy guy."

"I never met him," Paul said. "Always wanted to. Spent quite a bit of time trying to find him when I got older, but gave up years ago." Paul's eyes darted around the screen. "My mother spoke about Frank often. She was a wonderful person. I adored her. She was African-American, very light skinned. My mother's father was a minister. He and her brother made sure Frank signed my birth certificate, made some kind of deal with him. My mother always said she was heartbroken when Frank left her." Paul sighed. His voice faded as he sat back in his chair.

"She told me that Frank asked her to pass as a white woman, with her light skin. He wanted her to move away from her family, to another city with him and to raise me as white. But my mother just couldn't do that, didn't want to leave her family. And when she refused, Frank left. She said it was the hardest decision she ever had to make and it broke her heart."

"Where did you grow up?" I asked, mesmerized by the complexity of Paul's story.

"We lived in Newark, New Jersey for a bit, then in New York City, 125th Street, the middle of Harlem, for a while. Then Connecticut. My mom and her sister raised me. We always lived in black neighborhoods and I went to black schools. Always I was the odd guy out, with my white skin. Never was accepted by the black kids. Not even by some of my black relatives."

"Eventually I went to Northeastern University in Boston. Ended up being a math and history teacher to make my living. I still sub at a high school now."

Paul had the kind face of a teacher. Open and direct, he seemed like a nice guy.

We ended our zoom call with plans to meet in person in several weeks. Callie and her husband and three children, who lived in Florida, had planned a vacation in San Diego long before finding her father or me. Paul and his daughter Brianna planned to fly down to join us.

Paul's story of wanting to finding his father reminded me of my sister Vicki's recently found half-brother Jerry, Louie's son, the son Louie abandoned when Jerry was two years old. Jerry had expressed those same feelings Paul had just spoken of, a longing to find his father, of trying but eventually giving up. Both my sister and I had biological fathers who abandoned their sons. Both she and I have half-brothers who suffered the consequences of our fathers' actions. Two very different stories, but the emotional scars seemed much the same.

I was struck by the way racism affected Paul's life and upbringing. His father wanted his mother to pass as white. How will the rest of the Ferrinos react when I tell them about my half-brother Paul and the fact that Frank had a relationship with an African-American woman? Except for Carol, I hadn't forged much of a relationship with any of my Italian cousins. Our infrequent phone conversations and the occasional zoom calls had been superficial. I'd befriended several cousins on Facebook and wondered at their reactions to my photos of Black Lives Matter rallies and immigrant-rights marches. I'd ignored their occasional posts supporting Donald Trump. After the initial flush of excitement of meeting my paternal relatives, it seemed we didn't have much in common after all. And the Covid-19 pandemic precluded any travel plans to meet in person to test my hunch.

Paul's story was another example of how a large force acting on our culture, namely the scourge of racism, affected the individual stories of my family members. Racism, sexism, patriarchy, capitalism – they had become major factors impossible to ignore as I continued to unravel my birth history.

Chapter 34

"Oooh," my cousin Carol drew out the syllable dramatically after I told her about my half-brother Paul and the revelation that Frank, not Ernie, was my biological father. Carol was the Italian cousin I'd been closest to, the person most responsible for welcoming me into the Ferrino family. I called to tell her the news before I approached Frank's other children from his marriage.

"Remember I told you our grandparents had a rocky marriage?" Carol followed up on her exclamation. "They were separated for a while. And our grandmother, Angiolina, she had an affair with her sister's husband. She had two kids by him, a son, Frank, and a daughter Dolly."

It took me a minute to absorb this latest twist.

"You mean Frank's father was not a Ferrino?" I asked.

"He wasn't," Carol confirmed, her words clipped. "Frank and Dolly's father was Salvatore Vavala. But our grandfather Vincenzo Ferrino and grandmother Angiolina got back together and they raised both Frank and Dolly as

Ferrinos. This is still a big family secret. Not many people know."

I wasn't a descendent of the Ferrino clan after all. More secrets and lies complicated my biological heritage. I thought I'd at least pinpointed where in Italy my ancestors came from. Apparently even that small victory was a mirage.

"What do you know about Salvatore Vavala?" I sighed, disheartened.

"Not much. I hardly knew him. He was Italian, a heavy-set man. I didn't like him. I'm not sure if he immigrated from Italy or was born in the US."

I took a deep breath. Ernie Ferrino wasn't even my full uncle. He was only related to me on my grandmother's side. How was it that his photo provoked so many "oh, I can definitely see the resemblance between you and him" responses from the many friends and relatives I'd shown it to?

"And Frank?" I asked Carol. "What do you know about him?"

"He was very handsome. Tall and dark-haired. He owned a dry-cleaners. Made a very good living."

I thought back to the high praise Carol had for Ernie when she told me about him the first time. She'd gushed about what a kind and generous guy he was, how he'd give the shirt off his back to help someone.

"Anything else?" I asked.

"No, not really," she said. "He was married and he and his wife had three kids. You met his two daughters on our zoom call that time."

"I'm a little nervous about calling them and telling them we're really half-sisters, not cousins," I said. "Do you have any advice for me?"

"Call Cathy. She's not as straight-laced as her sister. And let me know how it goes."

*

The absurdity of the story hit me. I wasn't related, paternally, to the Ferrino clan after all! My grandmother, in the late 1940s, had an affair with her sister's husband. The Italian side of my family had secrets and lies of their own. The old daytime soap operas *The Days of Our Lives* and *General Hospital* had nothing compared to the saga that was my family history. My family lineage and roots were a farce, a slap-stick comedy.

I pulled up my Ancestry.com account and searched the name Vavala for DNA matches. Several very distant cousins had a Vavala in their family trees. Did I even want to go down that rabbit hole? Did I care? I closed my laptop.

*

"I've got some news," I started my phone conversation with Cathy, Frank's daughter, tentatively. "It turns out that your father was also my father and you and I are really half-sisters." I struggled to get the words out, worried about her reaction. My world had been turned upside down by all the revelations in my paternal history. I didn't relish putting someone else through any confusion and pain. Still, I did want to know a bit about my biological father, what kind of man he was. I wanted to see a picture of him at the age he'd met my mother. Hopefully Cathy would fill me in, and send me photos.

"I thought Ernie was your father," she said, her words terse. I explained all the twists and turns of the last several weeks, finding Paul, his birth certificate with Frank's signature, the unmistakable half-sibling DNA proof between Paul and me.

"Frank was an amazing dad. It's hard to imagine he had secrets as big as having other kids." I heard the disbelief in Cathy's voice. "How can you be so sure?"

I repeated the story.

"My mother dated Frank for only six months before they married," Cathy's tone shifted, became hesitant and questioning. "He was born in 1922, so he was twenty-eight when they married. He died when he was eighty, nineteen years ago, right before their fiftieth anniversary. His middle name was Paul." Her last sentence landed heavy with meaning. Paul was his first son's name. Paul was our half-brother.

"My dad never knew his exact birthday," Cathy said. "It was either the fourth or fifth of September. There was always something weird about his history and he hardly ever talked about his parents."

I hadn't been certain I'd spill the beans on our grandparents, the fact that our grandfather was Salvatorre Vavala and not Vincenzo Ferrino. But here was an opportunity to clear up a mystery for Cathy, so I took a deep breath and told her about the affair our grandmother had with her sister's husband.

"We're not even Ferrinos?" she said, her voice rising as she realized the implication of my words. "I always liked being a Ferrino. Remember the Hulk? The bodybuilder who was Mr. Universe? My family loved him. His real name was Lou Ferrigno, the way our grandpa used to like to spell his name. Now you're saying he wasn't even our grandpa, right?"

"It's all a lot to take in at once, isn't it?" I confirmed the news. Silence filled the miles between us for several seconds.

"What you're saying explains a lot about my family," Cathy said with a sigh. "We never spent any time with my dad's parents or that side of the family, except for Dolly." Dolly was Frank's only sibling whose father was actually Salvatorre Vavala. "There was always something fishy, something unspoken. I don't think my mother even knows the real story."

"I know that feeling of something just under the surface, something weird that you just can't put your finger on," I said. "All the secrets and lies. As for me, I'm glad the truth is finally coming out."

"One thing that doesn't change is that my dad was a great guy," Cathy said emphatically.

"He looked like Dean Martin, really handsome. I know he really loved us. And he worked very hard to give us a good life. He started out as a medic in the military. I have a photo of him in his uniform. I'll dig it out and send it to you."

We made plans for a zoom call later in the day. Cathy wanted to fill her sister Joan in on the news and include her on the call. I felt positive about our connection and told Cathy I looked forward to more conversations. But Joan was too busy to meet and we never scheduled the zoom call. I texted Cathy a few photos of myself and my mother. She sent me a photo of Frank as an elderly man and promised to send more later. I knew I needed to step back, give her and her family time to process the news. Wait for them to contact me. Wait. I was a pro at waiting.

*

Handsome. Frank was very handsome. The words from each of my conversations with my Italian cousin Carol and my new half-sister Cathy reverberated through me.

"I had a boyfriend once," my mother had told me years before. I remembered her emphasis on the 'I'. "He was very handsome," she'd said. My mother, in her early eighties, had been standing next to the piano in my dining room, watching me set the table for dinner. We'd been talking about my son Eli and a young woman he was dating. "I had a boyfriend before Louie," my mother said. "When I was young."

"Tell me more," I said, looking up to see a dreamy look in her eye, the signs of aging on her face smoothed away as memory swept her back to her youth.

"He was very handsome," she repeated, emphasis on the "very", a coy smile on her lips.

"You were drop-dead gorgeous too when you were young," I said. "Were you still in Germany when you met him? Or in New York?"

She hesitated a few seconds, turned away from me and headed toward the kitchen.

"New York," she said, her words terse.

"What happened? Did you two date very long?"

"Not really. We were young. Things happened and then didn't happen." My mother's back was to me and she bustled with the silverware.

"But you liked him?" I probed, puzzled by the sudden change in her demeanor, the softness of nostalgia replaced by a stiffened spine. "How did you meet?" I called after her.

"I don't remember," she said, not turning around. Eli and Walter walked into the room and the conversation shifted.

I recounted my memory of our mother and her handsome boyfriend to my sister Vicki during a phone call a few hours after I'd spoken with my half-sister Cathy.

"She told me that story several times," Vicki said. "How handsome he was. How he wined and dined her at the Rainbow Room." The Rainbow Room was a swanky restaurant on the top floor of Rockefeller Plaza on Fifth Avenue in Manhattan. "We laughed about how she ended up marrying Louie, the guy who took her to the automat."

Was my mother remembering Frank that evening in my dining room? Did she catch herself before spilling the rest of the story? Yes, I told myself. I had come very close to learning the truth that evening.

*

I pulled out the notes I'd taken during my conversation with Cathy. Frank married Cathy's mother in the summer of 1952. They'd dated for six months before they married. I did the math. I would have been between six to eight months old when Frank married. Either newborn or two months old when he'd met his future wife. Now I knew. My biological father had never been a part of my life. He may have known of my existence, but I had not formed any attachment with him. I never missed him when he left. I could lay those questions to rest.

I looked at the photo Cathy had texted me. It's a close-up of an old man, thick-jowled, with the ruddy complexion of a golfer who spent a lot of time in the sun. He stared back at me, his eyes wide behind horned-rim glasses. His head is cocked to one side and his lips are parted, exposing his upper teeth, the white of which match the bright white, collared oxford shirt unbuttoned at his throat.

No goosebumps tingled my arms. No surge of kinship zinged up my spine. My face wasn't reflected in his. He was just some guy. And there was just a hollow pit in my stomach.

*

The sturm und drang of the past weeks wreaked havoc with my sleep. My father wasn't Ernie, he was Frank. I'm not from the Ferrino clan, but some unknown, shady Vavala fellow; more intrigue, more drama. I rocked Cathy's world with all that news, and for what? Hadn't I deduced that patriarchy was behind my need to find my father? Why did I need to see a photo of Frank? I felt shame, guilt that I told Cathy, embarrassed that I'd made a big deal out of nothing. What difference did it all make anyway? I blamed myself for catastrophizing the story, dramatizing, demanding attention.

I didn't create this mess, another part of my brain countered. I didn't make up this convoluted story. I may not have handled it correctly. I may have made mistakes. My motivation was to find out a bit about what Frank was like, to get a photo of him in his twenties, when he knew my mother. My meditation tapes encouraged me to find self-compassion in my situation.

At core was still the three-year-old girl inside of me. The little girl who had to deal with an "all-of-a-sudden" daddy. A mommy who paid attention to him instead of me. A strange new daddy who didn't much care for me. A daddy who locked me in a closet.

Was I still trying to find my real Daddy, a Daddy who cared? The Daddy I never had? No matter my understanding of the historical roots of patriarchy, no matter my philosophizing that patriarchy was responsible for the romanticization of fatherhood and the paternal bloodline. The fact was, I was born into this culture where the nuclear family reigns and fathers are important and all my brain synapses were primed to respond to the stimulus of "Daddy". My internal wiring was at war with itself. I wanted a "Daddy" and I didn't want to want him.

I'd called Cathy to grab hold of this Daddy, a scrap of him, a photo, a life raft. There is no Daddy out there, I told myself. No picture will help. It's all a house of cards. Fake. Meaningless. I shook up a stable family – Cathy's – for what? She was no more my sister than my new neighbor next door. I was embarrassed I involved her. I'd jumped, rashly, into the drama of the moment. I couldn't undo my actions.

Could I find compassion for myself, for the emotional, re-active me that jumped into the fray, for the me that never asked for this drama but was in the middle of it nevertheless? A photograph of myself, little Gina, came to mind. The first photograph of Louie and me together, little Gina sitting on the grass with Louie, him looking away from me, aloof and distant. My scrunched-up, baffled, angry face. That girl, and myself in the present moment – we never asked for all the drama inherent in our story. Tears streaming down my cheeks, I wrapped little Gina snug in my arms and rocked us both to sleep.

*

Early the next morning sunlight lit the leaves on the juniper tree outside my office window and warmed my cheek. A pair of doves, recent residents under the eaves, cooed a greeting.

Drowsy from a poor night's sleep, a cup of steaming green tea before me, I breathed in the sunlight, breathed out the turmoil of the past few weeks. Breathe in, one, two, three, four, five. Breathe out, one, two, three, four, five. Hot tears in my eyes. Damp heat rolled up from my thighs to the roots of my hair, puddling under my arms.

In, one, two, three, four, five. Out, one, two, three, four, five.

My mother appeared before me. She's young and it's the summer I began my menstrual period on a trip to Taxco, Mexico. She leans against a palm tree, wearing a dress with a wide, white leather belt encircling her waist, pleated gingham falling to just below her knees. A cigarette, poised inches from her dusky pink lips, held taut between her index and middle finger. I can't make out her eyes behind her dark sunglasses. I can't quite guess her mood. She drops the cigarette, twists the toe of her white pump to grind it out, takes off her sunglasses. Her hazel eyes bore into mine.

"Here is your truth," her words echo with deep canyon resonance. "You were always wanted." Draped over her outstretched arms, like the vestments of a priest, is the alphabet tapestry her mother made in the Polish convent. My grandmother's tapestry that hangs on my dining room wall. I'm not surprised at my mother's change in appearance. She always did have the ability to shift on a dime.

I breathed in truth, one, two, three, four, five. Breathed out confusion. The truth was, it didn't matter what the truth was, who my mother had sex with, which brother, which dick, which guy either wanted her or didn't want her, which guy knew or didn't know she got pregnant. The truth was, it didn't matter who did or didn't bring his ear to her protruding belly to marvel at my fetal foot pushing against the boundary of her uterus, whether or not his hands cupped the swollen proof of my existence. The truth was, it didn't matter whether he held or didn't hold me, cocooned in a swaddling blanket, that nine pounds of me my mother blamed on eating too much butter with radishes during her pregnancy. The truth was, I gurgled and cooed and learned to roll over – all of that happened, whether or not he was a witness to my existence. The truth was, I was still me, today, regardless of any new revelations. I still walked the California shoreline. I still wrote. I still longed for the solace of the Sierra. One thing that had changed since embarking on the journey to find my paternal family, ironically, was my realization of the primal, deep connection between my mother and me. The rest of the characters - Louie, Ernie, Frank - seemed superfluous. My identity began with my mother, with an ovum in her ovary. She's the one I've been seeking since I set out to unravel the mystery of why I was never told the truth about my beginnings.

I breathed in strength, the strength of my mother's will to survive as she stood on the deck of a refugee freighter witnessing bombs exploding around her, her cunning to endure displaced persons camps, her resolve to end her life on her own terms.

I breathed in the strength of all the mothers who came before me. Heat rose in my body. The heat of anger. Not sadness. Not confusion. The righteous rage of the Hindu goddess Kali, birthed from her mother's forehead to slay the demons haunting her domain. The righteous anger of the women marching in yesterday's rally to defend a woman's right to reproductive choice, chanting "We won't go back!" "Our bodies, Our choice." "Mind your own uterus!" The righteous anger of women around the globe demanding an end to gender violence.

I breathed in power. My individual journey was part of the collective history of female experience. My sisters lead the evolution of humanity toward a better world. My home was in that struggle.

Chapter 35

I met face-to-face with my half-brother Paul in the lobby of a Hampton Inn near the San Diego airport. He and his daughter Brianna had flown in from Washington the night before.

I recognized the hair and build of the man walking toward me from our zoom call weeks before. A white t-shirt pulled taut across his belly.

"Gina?" he asked behind his Covid-appropriate face mask. "Should I take it off?" He pulled at his mask.

"I want to see all of you," I said as I took mine off and stopped a couple of feet in front of him.

Paul stuck out his hand.

"I want a hug," I said and pulled him close, breaking all Covid rules.

"So weird," he said as we loosened our grip, stepped back. "This. All of this." His arms flailed the air as his voice trailed off.

"I know," I said. "Important, yet who are we really to each other, with just this DNA connection?" I took a chance with honesty.

"So glad you said that," Paul looked directly into my eyes. "Spoke to the elephant in the room. You broke the ice."

We pushed chairs in the hotel lobby close together, the desk registry staff eyeing us as our voices echoed off the high ceiling and glass windows. We sat down and began our journey towards becoming family.

Our conversation and laughter flowed freely, the oddity of our situation giving us plenty to talk about. I felt at ease with this brother-man. After an hour we all piled into our car to join Paul's newly-found daughter, Callie, her husband and their three children at their beach-front AirBnB.

I witnessed a daughter greet her biological father. For some, an everyday event. For Callie, an earth-shattering moment. "It will take me weeks to process this," Callie confided to me later in the day. I witnessed a father and daughter embrace, their first embrace. I witnessed their eyes lock. Their tears. Their obvious facial resemblance.

I will never meet my biological father. Deep in my body this fact registered again and again.

I witnessed a grandfather, my brother Paul, hug his three grandchildren for the first time, his ten-year-old granddaughter with a head of curls. "Just like my mother's", Paul said.

My mind swirled with conflicted thoughts. Who were these people to me really? We had no history, no touchpoints.

Our touchstone, what we had in common, was that Paul, Callie and I weren't raised by our biological fathers. That exposed wound opened a vulnerability in us. That was our bond. It stoked an intimacy between us, infused the emotional tenor of our afternoon together. We'd just met, yet our conversations were deep and personal.

Side by side, Paul and I had the same shape face, a similar cut of jaw, high forehead. When we put two photos of us taken when we were each in our twenties side by side, our facial features popped with resemblance. We were cut of the same cloth in our youth, before his paunch, his close-cut white/grey beard, my sag and wrinkles. We'd morphed and matured into our current state based on those foundations.

My brother was emotional, quick to tear up, transparent with his love for his daughter Brianna, who he raised as a single father. He was warm, quick to embrace Callie and me. He arrived at Callie and her family's Airbnb with a box of chocolate chip cookies he'd baked the day before. He was a good guy, that was clear. He was self-deprecating in that funny way of people with a good sense of humor. And smart. He was a book reader, we had that in common. Our world outlook, our politics meshed. The two of us, raised apart from our biological paternal roots, evolved into people much different than the Ferrinos I'd met who were raised in the Italian, Catholic fold. I liked my brother. We could easily be friends. I didn't feel any of the male/female sexual tension often present in opposite sex interactions. On a beach walk with the family that afternoon he and I bumped up against each other, laughed, linked eyes and hip-bumped each other again. Goofed around. I'd never felt a male/female bond like that. I just plain liked the guy and the more I got to know him, the more I wanted him in my life.

We lamented the fact that we lived so far apart, Paul in eastern Washington, me in San Diego. Paul made plans to visit Callie and her family in Florida and we all promised to stay in touch. We'd had a joyous beginning to our new found family and neither of us wanted to say goodbye.

*

My body shut down the day after I met my half-brother and nieces. Even after a welcome eight hours of sleep, I was exhausted, weighted down, lethargic and head-achy. Was it Covid? Or did my body know the importance of the day before, the meeting of my brother, the bond of our heritage, the weight of our connection? My body, by slowing me down, by pinning me to the sofa, insisted I honor the gravity of the occasion, this meeting of my kin.

It mattered that I have a half-brother, that his father was the man who provided the sperm to fertilize my mother's ovum. In my body and mind, primed by the forces of the culture of my upbringing, it mattered. Yet our brother-sister connection was illusive, like passing my hand through steam. I could see the vapor, yet my hand cut right through.

Frank's two daughters born of his marriage, my biological half-sisters, never answered the many texts I sent after our first telephone conversation. I imagined they wanted nothing to do with me or Paul, uncomfortable reminders of their father's not-so-illustrious past. Although dismayed they never sent me a photo of Frank as a young man, the man who would have been my mother's "handsome boyfriend", I didn't much lament our disconnection. We probably had little in common anyway.

I already felt close to my half-brother Paul and my two nieces. I wondered where our relationship would evolve from here.

Chapter 36

In the months following our new family get-together, Paul texted a "Happy Sunday" greeting each Sunday to Callie, Brianna and I, often with a photo of his latest culinary concoction of cauliflower crust pizza or zucchini lasagna. He was trying to cut down on carbs to deal with his diabetes. Some Sundays he'd just send a photo of a sunset. But every Sunday I could count on his text, a reminder he was thinking of me. A reminder I had a brother out there in the world.

In my replies to him I always wrote "Hi Paul", not "Hi, Brother". He usually called me "Sis". We had a few telephone conversations and I invited him to stay with Walter and me in San Diego each time. He'd make a plan and then cancel it. At seventy-one years old, he was still substitute teaching at a high school. He told me he needed the money and that also he needed to feel useful, to have something to do.

Late October rolled around, ten months since we'd met, and I realized a couple of months had passed since we'd talked on the phone. I wanted to hear his voice. And I wanted to deepen our relationship. Thanksgiving was on the horizon and Walter and I hoped Paul and his daughter Briana would join us for dinner at our house.

Something had shifted in me and I was ready to open my heart to the fact of our kinship. I wanted to embrace Paul, call him Brother, regardless of whether we were raised apart and never knew we existed until last year. I imagined we'd walk the beach together, the early evening San Diego sky lit up in purple, pink and orange glory. We'd talk, really talk, about this strange twist of fate we'd both experienced, this father who hadn't been our father, the oddity of a DNA connection showing up on our faces all these years later. We'd marvel at our luck in finding each other in the sunset of our lives. I had a big brother, a male confidant, a guy who loved me without conditions. And I could be his sister.

When Paul's usual "Happy Sunday" text arrived, I replied "Hey, Brother, I'd love to hear your voice and have a phone conversation soon…do you have any time tomorrow?" And we made a plan to talk the next day.

My cell phone buzzed in the morning and Paul's name lit up the screen.

"Hi, Paul," I said, so happy he'd called.

Instead of Paul's voice, I heard "This is Brianna." Why would Paul's daughter be calling me on Paul's phone?

"I'm calling with bad news," Brianna's words sounded slow and elongated.

"Oh no. What happened?" I reached for a chair to catch the sudden tremendous weight at the center of my body, my legs like jelly.

"My father died last night," Brianna's voice cracked a pistol shot staccato across the miles between us.

Whoosh, all the oxygen left the room. "No, no, not possible. We were going to talk this morning," I choked out. I was going to open up to him, claim him, call him my brother.

"He collapsed in an aisle at Safeway," Brianna said. "An ambulance took him to the hospital and he died in the ER. They think he had a massive heart attack."

Brianna and I were both sobbing. She was only twenty-two years old. Paul was her only parent. I had waited too long to pursue a closer connection with my brother. Now it was too late.

"I'm so sorry," I kept repeating. When I asked if she needed help making the funeral arrangements, Brianna said she'd let me know.

*

Callie, Paul's older daughter, was crying when she answered my call. She'd had less than a year with her newly-found biological father.

"He just sent me a check to buy Christmas presents for my kids," she said. "We were in touch almost every day. I was beginning to trust he'd always be there for us."

We made plans to share a hotel room near the funeral home in Walla Walla, Washington where Paul's service would be held.

"Paul told me many times that he was so happy Brianna had a big sister now," Callie said. "He asked me to look out for her if something happened to him."

*

The clouds in the sky on my three-hour drive from the Spokane airport to Walla Walla looked like a baker with a giant knife had iced a cake above me, rolled and swirled long swaths in every shade of white and gray and black. Wheat fields, cut down now in late autumn, undulated in mixed hues of yellow and tan, brown and black. I drove my rental car on the roller coaster of gentle hills and curves, going miles without seeing another car, then rounding a bend to see a silo, sky-scraper high, cut the distance between me and the clouds. Tumbling boulders appeared in the distance and as I got closer they morphed into stacks of hay bales, moldy and crumbling, falling into and over themselves, remnants of an earlier harvest. Each new vista expanded into an alien landscape, immense and majestic.

On and on, grays and umbers, until an expanse of neon green appeared on a rise to my left. Beyond it the solid ground collapsed into a canyon. Up ahead a train trestle, scaffolds of steel, ten-stories high, cut the valley along a wide, rushing river. Then, shimmering in the far distance, impossibly, an ocean of white-capped waves, later revealed to be a snow- covered mountain range.

The gorgeous, rugged landscape split my heart wide open.

*

I sat between my two nieces on the first row of chairs at the funeral home, the three of us holding hands. Brianna had gathered memorabilia from Paul's life – his golf clubs, a floppy, gray Titleist hat, an oil painting of his mother, his PhD Dissertation, his wallet and keys – now on display in front of us.

Paul's cousins and their families and Brianna's friends were there, too. His high school students, at least twenty-five of them, filled the back seats. Several of them gave heartfelt tributes after the pastor's generic eulogy.

"Mr. Ferrino is why I'm sober today," said one young man. Jet black hair cascaded down his back. His suit looked like it was made for a guy half his height and twice his width, the black material slick and shiny with wear. "He was there for me, for all of us," he said. "Mr. Ferrino was just the best. He always came into our classroom with a big smile."

Three young women walked to the dais together, bumping up next to each other, standing close on the narrow platform.

"He was like a father to me," one said, choking back tears. "I can't believe he won't be in class tomorrow." She turned toward her friend and inched the mic under her chin.

"He always made me feel like I mattered to him," the second young woman said, swishing long bangs across her forehead. "I'm really going to miss him."

I learned about Paul's life by talking with his cousins at the gathering after the funeral. He'd been a drug user of crack and cocaine until twenty-two years ago when his daughter Brianna was born. Knowing he couldn't trust Brianna's mother to get sober, he went to rehab for twenty-eight days after his daughter's birth, got clean and then raised her as a single father.

He got a law degree in his fifties, but, unsuccessful in finding a position as an attorney, he kept working as a high school math teacher.

Longing to get more of a tangible sense of Paul, some way to fill the hole in my gut when I realized, over and over, that I was never going to lay eyes on him again, I asked Brianna to take me to Paul's apartment. On the way there we drove by the Safeway where he collapsed. It had been Halloween night, and I imagined he'd been shopping for candy for the kids in his neighborhood. I imagined Mars Bars and Snickers strewn on the tile floor, the bright fluorescent lights glaring, the thud of his body. The panicked voices of the other shoppers. I imagined his confusion and chagrin at causing a ruckus. He'd never liked drawing attention to himself. He was a giver, not a receiver.

He lived in a run-down apartment complex in the poor part of town, in Oregon, near the border of Washington, because, as Brianna explained, the rents were much cheaper than in the tonier college town of Walla Walla. Mold and stale cigarette smoke filled my nose as I climbed the stairs to his door. Inside, his place was a mess – pots, pans and dishes in the sink, layers of dust, windows too grimy to see through.

But the defining feature of his place was the piles of books everywhere, the brick and plywood bookshelves lined with books, his bedside table stacked with books, books and more books, mostly non-fiction – law books, books on imaginary math, political and sociology books. At Brianna's urging I kept two from the shelve under the window, "Caste: The Origins of Our Discontents" by Isabel Wilkerson and "The Color of Law: A Forgotten History of How Our

Government Segregated America" by Richard Rothstein, both titles I'd been meaning to pick up myself. I also kept the gray, floppy Titleist hat that had been at the funeral home the day before.

*

Callie and I had each come to Walla Walla for four days. Paul's funeral came and went in a day's time, leaving us many hours to fill. Walla Walla was a quintessential picturesque college town, with a Main Street of refurbished old brick buildings, lined with red maple and Raywood ash trees in an autumn splendor of amber and red leaves, their trunks encircled in festive, tiny white lights. The intermittent rain and cold wind couldn't dampen the charm of the town and the warmth of the hours Callie and I spent together, searching out ethnic restaurants, perusing the display window of a bookstore, all the while talking, talking, talking. Into the late night we'd sprawled on our side-by-side queen beds in our small hotel room, sharing details of our lives.

Brianna and I had less time together, but it was no less poignant. She also clearly wanted a close relationship with me, happy to call me "auntie". We fantasized about taking a trip to Italy together to the birthplace of our ancestors.

*

Paul's light had gone to ground, his corporeal body reduced to ash. My deep grief over his death stirred up the despair I'd felt over the past four and a half years – all the emotional pain of unraveling the lies, all the twists and turns of finding my biological paternal family – and in the weeks after the funeral I struggled to regain my equilibrium.

Who could Paul and I have been for each other had abandonments, lies and deceptions not kept us apart? If only he'd been there to yank open the door when I was three years old and locked in the closet. What would having a sister have meant to him when he was growing up? I would never know.

*

Four months after the funeral, during a late-night zoom call, Callie and I reminisced about our time together in Walla Walla.

"It was so strange, the juxtaposition of being devastated by Paul's death alongside the joy I felt in being with you," Callie said, echoing my feelings exactly. My nieces were now firmly woven into the fabric of my family and I treasured our relationship.

The next morning, I hiked the eastern hills of San Diego, the slopes dazzling with spring's bounty of bright orange California poppies and purple lupine. Lilac flowers on ceanothus bushes popped against green leaves. I craned my neck to decipher the culprits of a cacophony of cawing above me; shiny blue-black ravens surfed wind currents through the canyon against a cerulean sky.

When, just a month before, I had walked the same trail, the landscape had been gray, the soil barren and soggy with a fetid scent of muck. Now each bush and flower bloomed miraculous, sprouted from the very same earth. The grit had made all the radiance possible.

References

Copeland, Libby. The Lost Family: How DNA Testing is Upending Who We Are. New York: Abrams Press, 2020.

Firestone, PhD, Rabbi Tirzah. Wounds into Wisdom: Healing Intergenerational Jewish Trauma. New York: Adam Kadmon Books/Monkfish Book Publishing Company, 2019.

Kluppel, Karolin. "Portraits of Matriarchy: Where Grandmothers Are Still in Charge". Yes! 9 Nov. 2020.

Lerner, Gerda. The Creation of Patriarchy. New York: Oxford University Press, 1986.

Nollendorfs, Valters, ed. Museum of the Occupation of Latvia: Latvia under the Rule of the Soviet Union and National Socialist Germany, 1940 – 1991. Riga, Latvia, 2002.

Reed, Evelyn. Woman's Evolution: From Matriarchal Clan to Patriarchal Family. New York: Pathfinder Press, 1975.

Rosenberg, Donna. World Mythology: An Anthology of the Great Myths and Epics. 2nd ed. Lincolnwood, IL: National Textbook, 1994.

Zhang, Sarah. "When a DNA Test Shatters Your Identity". Atlantic 17 July 2018.

Zimmer, Carl. She Has Her Mother's Laugh: The Powers, Perversions, and Potential of Heredity. New York: Dutton, 2018.

Acknowledgements

I was a lucky woman to have the willing ear and support of family and friends during the evolution of this memoir. Many walks and talks with Walter Cameron, Eli Cameron, Libbie Brydolf, Elisabeth Lohse, Barbara Cohen and Janice Sams-Cespedes helped me sift through my jumbled thoughts and feelings as I tried to make sense of the events herein. Also invaluable was the attentive listening of my peer-counselors Mannie Garza, Vilma Palencia, Ahouva Steinhaus and Blair Overstreet.

Many thanks to my life-long friend and writing partner Sonja Franeta for the many zoom meetings where we shared our lives and our writing and for your early critiques of my work.

Judy Reeves, my writing mentor and friend, has been an inspiration as a writer, human being and creator of writing community since she opened the San Diego Writing Center in the early 1990s. The seeds of this memoir were generated in Judy's "Wild Women Writing" workshop and in countless classes, workshops and conversations over coffee since. No words can express the depth of my gratitude.

Tish Sjoberg and her Expressive Arts Studio gave me creative encouragement and space to expand my fledgling artist self. Many thanks to the writers in the Wednesday morning Writers Support Group - Tish, Trudy, Patricia, Niyazi, Judith and Nancy and to the artists in our Visual Journaling Group - Alice, Marianne, Paula, Therese, Patricia, Janice and Tish.

San Diego Writers, Ink has been an anchor for me and hundreds of writers since a few friends and I sat around a dining room table in 2003 and launched our dream of a physical space for our writing community. It has grown and blossomed beyond our wildest imagination. Many thanks to Steve Montgomery and Judy Reeves for continuously stoking the fires of the "Thursday Writers" drop-in group and for your provocative writing prompts, many of which inspired scenes in my book.

My memoir got a big boost when I joined the online class "Write Your Memoir in 6 Months" during the depths of the pandemic. Many thanks to my first editor, Linda Joy Myers, for your early guidance. I was lucky to be partnered during the class with San Diego writer Linda Black, who has since become a friend and writing collaborator.

When the scenes and chapters of this book languished in disorganized computer files, Joey Edwards stepped in with his reassuring presence and computer wizardry. Thanks so much for your patience and support.

Thank you to my beta readers Judy Anderson, Sonja Franeta and Elisabeth Lohse. Your feedback made my book better. And thanks again to Elisabeth Lohse for your eagle eye and patience to edit my final (almost!) draft.

Thank you to Robert Burroughs for your excellence as a photographer and for taking the time to give my book a beautiful cover.

I am grateful for the guidance of Katie Dove, teacher, healer and wise woman. Your presence kept me centered through the turbulence of this journey.

Thank you to Kali Kucera for sharing your skills as a publishing consultant and book midwife. It was a pleasure working with you.

Thank you to Shawn Cameron, Tara Cameron and James Cameron for all the richness your presence has brought to our extended family. And thanks to my sister Vicki for always infusing our time spent together with your boundless sense of merriment.

My heart swells with gratitude as I write these pages and once again realize how many people contributed to the making of this book. Even so, it still would not have been possible without the unwavering support and love from my husband, Walter.

My son, Eli, is my greatest gift and constant source of inspiration. As always, I love being your mother!

Gina Cameron

Who's My Daddy?

Gina Cameron

Printed in the USA
CPSIA information can be obtained
at www.ICGtesting.com
LVHW021635110624
782954LV00009B/553

9 798218 353728